biz
COMMON SENSE

Rachel Somer

UPPER LEVEL

DARAKWON

Biz
COMMON
SENSE UPPER LEVEL

Author Rachel Somer
Publisher Chung Kyudo
Editors Kwak Bitna, Cho Sangik
Designers Park Bohee, Jeong Kyuok
Photo Credit pg. 50 (brand) Bloomicon

First Published April 2021
By Darakwon Inc.
Darakwon Bldg., 211, Munbal-ro, Paju-si, Gyeonggi-do 10881
Republic of Korea

Tel. 82-2-736-2031 (Ext. 552)

Price ₩14,000
ISBN 978–89–277–0988–6 14740
      978–89–277–0986–2 14740 (set)

http://www.darakwon.co.kr

Main Book / Free MP3 Available Online
7 6 5 4 3 2 1   21 22 23 24 25

Introduction

Biz Common Sense—12 Workplace Missions in English for Upper-level Professionals is designed for readers who wish to improve their English language skills for a professional environment. The book allows readers to experience situations that commonly occur on the job and provides meaningful guidance for responding to these situations.

The book is divided into twelve missions. Each mission includes three situations that focus on one typical scenario or problem that can occur in an upper-level business position. The situations are presented in a variety of formats, such as emails, conversations, telephone calls, voicemails, text messages, group chats, schedules, and notices.

Readers should begin each mission by reading Situation 1 and by answering some questions. This section is followed by background knowledge about the mission topic and a vocabulary exercise. Following that, readers practice a dialogue related to the topic and complete a one-page grammar lesson. Situation 2, which responds to Situation 1 with additional information, is presented next. Readers then learn a variety of relevant expressions before concluding the mission with Situation 3.

This book is ideal for classrooms, study groups, and individuals. Readers can complete the missions in any order they like. However, it is recommended that they complete all three situations in each mission before moving on. Completing each mission in full will give readers a greater understanding of problem-solving in an English-language workplace.

I would like to express my gratitude to Kwak Bitna, the editor of this book, as well as the entire Darakwon team. Their constant support made the development of this book possible.

I hope readers find this book useful in preparing them for real-world business situations. Solving problems in English can be overwhelming, but by studying the missions in this book, readers can gain the tools they need to feel confident in the workplace.

Rachel Somer

Scope and Sequence

Mission	Background Knowledge	Vocabulary
01 **Recruiting New Employees** p.8	How to recruit new employees	Parts of a résumé
02 **Welcoming New Employees** p.16	Orientation sessions	People and activities at orientation sessions
03 **Conducting a Survey** p.24	Ways to conduct surveys	Survey topics
04 **Getting an Overseas Assignment** p.32	International assignments	Words related to international assignments
05 **Planning a Charity Event** p.40	How to plan a charity event	Charity events
06 **Dealing with Complaints** p.48	Dealing with customer complaints	Words related to customer complaints

Grammar	Expressions
Prepositions of time	Mentioning a recommendation Mentioning a candidate's work experience Mentioning your own work experience Concluding an interview
Uses of *do*	Acknowledging someone's efforts Acknowledging your team's efforts Referencing prior information Making a compromise
Direct and indirect questions	Expressing gratitude with a request Providing an incentive with instructions Asking about frequency Asking about a preference
Quantifiers	Delivering good news Responding to good news Informing someone of an appointment Providing further instructions
To-infinitives to show the purpose of an action	Proposing a possible solution Accepting or rejecting a proposed solution Adding contradictory information Asking for advice
The present perfect continuous tense	Starting a meeting Giving employees assignments Replying to orders Volunteering to solve a problem

Mission	Background Knowledge	Vocabulary
07 **Preparing for a Sales Meeting** p.56	Sales meetings	Words related to sales meetings
08 **Moving to a New Office** p.64	Reasons for moving to a new office	Words related to moving
09 **Getting a Promotion** p.72	Getting a promotion	Positions at a company
10 **Asking for a Raise** p.80	Asking for a raise	Words related to asking for a raise
11 **Being Nominated for an Award** p.88	Selecting the employee of the year	Words related to awards ceremonies
12 **Resigning** p.96	Giving notice when resigning	Words related to resigning

Grammar	Expressions
Collocations: *give*, *make*, and *take*	Changing topics during a presentation Explaining a drastic change Drawing attention to data Making conclusions
Must and *have to*	Asking for an estimate Making an estimate Delivering bad news Responding to bad news
Sense verbs	Asking about availability Acknowledging effort Responding to praise humbly Returning praise
The present perfect tense	Following up after an agreement Mentioning consequences Saying goodbye informally Responding to an informal goodbye
Can	Providing advice Expressing anticipation Offering congratulations to a winner Responding to congratulations
To-infinitives as object complements	Asking for more information about a problem Making a concession Expressing understanding Expressing confusion

Recruiting New Employees

Situation ❶

A Walter Jones is discussing a staffing issue with his coworker, Janette Ellis. Read the telephone conversation. 🔊 01-1

📞 **Walter Jones** Hi, Janette. This is Walter Jones from management calling.

📞 **Janette Ellis** Hi, Mr. Jones. What can I do for you?

📞 **Walter Jones** I'm not sure if your team in the Human Resources Department got the news yet, but we're going to expand the Sales Department.

📞 **Janette Ellis** That's great to hear.

📞 **Walter Jones** Yes, the sales team did a great job last quarter. We have a lot of new clients, so we're going to need more staff members to handle their accounts.

📞 **Janette Ellis** Would you like me to start posting some job advertisements?

📞 **Walter Jones** Yes. We need at least two sales representatives. They should be able to maintain good client relationships. In addition, two years of experience in a sales position is preferable.

📞 **Janette Ellis** When would you like them to start?

📞 **Walter Jones** Training starts in mid-May.

📞 **Janette Ellis** Okay. I'll collect applications until April 20 then. I'll also attend Richmond University's job fair next week. That will be a great chance to recruit new graduates.

📞 **Walter Jones** That's an excellent idea.

Pop-up Questions

1 What department does Ms. Ellis work in?

2 Why does the company need to hire more staff members?

3 Who will place some job advertisements?

4 Where will Ms. Ellis go next week?

B **Take Notes ::** **Based on the conversation in A, complete the job posting.**

Position Sales Representative   **Posted** April 4 at 10:38 A.M.

Responsibilities

Sell company products to new and existing clients and ¹ _____

Qualifications

- BS/BA degree and ² _____

- Excellent written and verbal communication skills

How to Apply

- Submit your résumé and application to ³ _____ in Human Resources by ⁴ _____

- Successful hires must be available to begin training in ⁵ _____

Background Knowledge

A **Read and learn about how to recruit new employees.**

Hiring new employees is a necessary part of business. The right employees can keep a business running successfully. But finding new staff members is not always easy. There are a few ways to successfully fill an open position.

First, consider existing employees. You might be able to fill a position by promoting someone. If that's not possible, ask for referrals. Your coworkers might recommend someone for the job. You could also ask former colleagues or other business contacts. They might know the perfect candidate for the position.

If referrals fail, you may have to rely on job postings. Place advertisements online or in newspapers. Interested candidates will submit applications and résumés. Invite qualified candidates to have interviews. Job fairs are also a great way to recruit. Many universities hold job fairs for recent graduates. Register to attend one and then meet potential employees in person.

Pop-up Questions

1 Why should you consider existing employees for an open position?

2 What will interested candidates submit?

B **Listen to the conversation and answer the questions.** 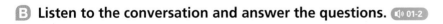 01-2

1 **Who works in the Human Resources Department?**

    a. Jeff   b. Margo   c. Theresa

2 **What is the company planning to do?**

    a. open a restaurant   b. host a job fair   c. fire the head chef

3 **When will Jeff go to the job fair?**

    a. today   b. next month   c. next year

Vocabulary

Complete the résumé by filling in the blanks with the following words: Experience, Skills, Education, References, Personal Summary, Post-secondary Institution.

Phillip Benson

IT Officer

1 _____

A hardworking and responsible professional with four years of experience in IT Support. A proven team player who has established effective work relationships. Highly organized and motivated with the ability to manage multiple tasks at once.

Work **2** _____

IT Officer

Blue Island Bank   2017 – 2020

- Provided technical support and consultations
- Managed banking systems and related applications
- Investigated customer reports and complaints
- Organized and led training seminars for new hires

Details

23 Coleman Road
Savannah, Georgia, 30713
(912) 223-7765
pbenson@mailme.com

3 _____

Bachelor of Computer Science, University of Redfern
September 2012 – June 2016   **4** _____

High School Diploma, Greenbriar High School
September 2008 – June 2012

5 _____

Database management
Hardware and software installation
Troubleshooting
Leadership
Conflict resolution

6 _____

Dan Alvarez, IT Manager, Blue Island Bank
danalvarez@blueislandbank.com 912-909-7700

Dr. Jennifer Wellington, University of Redfern
jenniferwellington@redfernu.com 912-887-3324

Speak Up

Practice the conversation with your partner by using the information in each job application. 01-3

(Example)

Name Roger Zhao
Phone 887-332-1120
Position Applied For Sales Representative
Education Bachelor of Arts in Business Management, Frasier University

Employment
- Company: Blackford Business Solutions
- Position: Sales Representative
- Dates: 2015 – 2020

(Application 1)

Name Jess Cordon
Phone 334-557-0907
Position Applied For Lead Architect
Education Master of Architecture, Cole University

Employment
- Company: the New Gold Development Company
- Position: Architect
- Dates: 2018 – 2020

(Application 2)

Name Leanne Buford
Phone 998-432-1298
Position Applied For Head Nurse
Education Bachelor of Science in Nursing, Freemont College

Employment
- Company: Hope Hospital
- Position: Nurse
- Dates: 2012 – 2019

(Application 3)

Name Isabella Ford
Phone 443-876-2231
Position Applied For Administrative Assistant
Education Associate Degree in Business Administration, Wellington Technical College

Employment
- Company: Drake Wilson Law
- Position: Administrative Assistant
- Dates: 2014 – 2021

A Hi, Mandy. Do you have a minute to look at an application?

B Sure. Let me see it.

A This is Roger Zhao's application.

B I see. He/She has a(n) bachelor of arts in business management.

A Yes, and he/she worked at Blackford Business Solutions.

B Wow, he/she was there for five years.

A That's right. I think we should call him/her for an interview.

B Wait. What position is he/she applying for?

A He's/She's interested in the sales representative position.

B Oh, I see. Yes, let's give him/her a call.

! Tips for Success

When assessing a job application, consider how long an employee worked at his or her previous employer.

GRAMMAR

A   Let's learn about prepositions of time.

at – for precise times	*in* – for long periods of time
The class is **at** 10:45 A.M. The presentation finishes **at** 4:00 P.M.	The position will open **in** December. He started the company **in** 2002.
on – for days and dates	*for* – for a period of time
The meeting is **on** Friday. Her vacation starts **on** July 6.	She worked there **for** ten years. The interview lasted **for** two hours.
during – when two things happen at the same time	*until* – to show the end of a period of time
They stayed at a hotel **during** the conference. He slept **during** his flight.	They talked on the phone **until** 6:00 P.M. She was his boss **until** he quit.

B   Complete the following sentences by using the correct prepositions of time.

1   The orientation session will begin _____ 9:30 A.M. tomorrow.

2   I'm not sure when the packages will arrive. Maybe _____ Thursday.

3   The client asked a lot of questions _____ his trip.

4   You have _____ next Friday to submit your application.

5   The CEO is thinking of attending the conference _____ February.

6   I worked at Dexter International _____ five years.

7   The fall hiring period starts _____ May 24.

8   The company merger happened in spring _____ 2008.

📶 Know-how *at* Work   **How to Behave with Potential Employees**

Having a professional attitude during a job interview is important. Some applicants will be offered multiple positions. Thus, you should present your company as the best choice.

1   When calling an applicant to schedule an interview, introduce yourself. Mention the name of your company and why you are calling. Offer the applicant at least two interview time slots.

2   If you must change an interview time, let the applicant know right away. Apologize for the inconvenience and offer a new interview time.

3   When the applicant arrives for the interview, greet him or her politely. Smile and offer him or her a seat. Don't make the applicant stay in a waiting room for too long.

4   During the interview, ask questions in a clear, direct manner. Don't use overly casual language. Stay on topic and listen carefully to the applicant's answers. Make sure to explain more about the position and the company as well.

Situation ②

Ⓐ **Walter Jones is interviewing an applicant, Willow Preston, for the sales representative position. Read the conversation.** ◁)) 01-4

W Have a seat, Ms. Preston. It's nice to meet you.

W Thank you, Mr. Jones. Please call me Willow.

W Certainly. Thank you for coming for a second interview. Janette Ellis in Human Resources highly recommended you for the sales representative position.

W That's great to hear.

W So I see you have three years of experience as a sales representative. Can you tell me about that?

W Of course. The company is Sandford Labs. It develops medical products. I was a junior sales representative for two years and then a team leader for one.

W I see. Why did you leave Sandford Labs?

W Well, the company is based in Chicago. I decided to move to L.A. to be closer to my family.

W And you're looking for a permanent full-time position?

W That's correct.

W Good to hear. I think you'll do a great job here.

W Thank you, Mr. Jones.

W The sales manager will arrive shortly. She has some additional questions for you.

Pop-up Questions

1 Who recommended Ms. Preston for the position?

2 Where did Ms. Preston used to work?

3 Why did Ms. Preston move to L.A.?

4 What type of position does Ms. Preston want?

Ⓑ **Problem Solving ::** **Walter Jones must call Willow Preston to explain that the job has been changed to a short-term contract position. Find a partner and choose the roles of Walter Jones and Willow Preston. Then, role-play to discuss a possible solution. Use the information from the conversation in A if necessary.**

 **Useful Expressions**

A **Let's learn some expressions to use in business.**

When mentioning a recommendation	When mentioning a candidate's work experience
Janette Ellis highly recommended you.	I see you have three years of experience.
Mr. Welsh spoke very highly of you.	I heard you worked at the Rich Institute for three years.
I've heard great things about you.	It seems you have a lot of experience.
You come highly recommended.	I noticed you were employed at Greenburg Law.
When mentioning your own work experience	**When concluding an interview**
I worked at the Zeno Corporation for five years.	I think you'll do a great job here.
I have ten years of experience as a researcher.	We'll be in touch soon.
I was the sales manager there for 4 years.	Thank you for coming in.

B **Fill in the blanks with the correct answers from the box. Then, practice the conversation with a partner.** 🔊 01-5

worked at Umber Securities for three years	Peter Umber spoke very highly of you
I think you'll do a great job here	I see you were also employed at Kent Investment

A Hi, Ms. Nita. Thanks for coming in for an interview.

B Of course. It's great to be here.

A ¹ _____ .

B Yes, I ² _____ .

A Why did you leave Umber Securities?

B Well, the main branch relocated to London. I decided not to move.

A ³ _____ .

B That's right. I really enjoyed working there.

A You have a lot of experience, Ms. Nita. ⁴ _____ .

B Thank you. I'm excited about the position.

A Great. Thanks for coming in. We'll be in touch soon.

Extra Practice

Role-play with your partner. An interviewer mentions a candidate's work experience. The candidate replies with more information.

A Patty Morgan spoke very highly of you.

B Yes, I worked at Morgan Designs for three years.

A I noticed you were also employed at Zone Graphics.

B That's right. I really enjoyed working there.

Situation 3

Willow Preston gets an email welcoming the new recruits to the company. Read the email and see if the results are positive or negative.

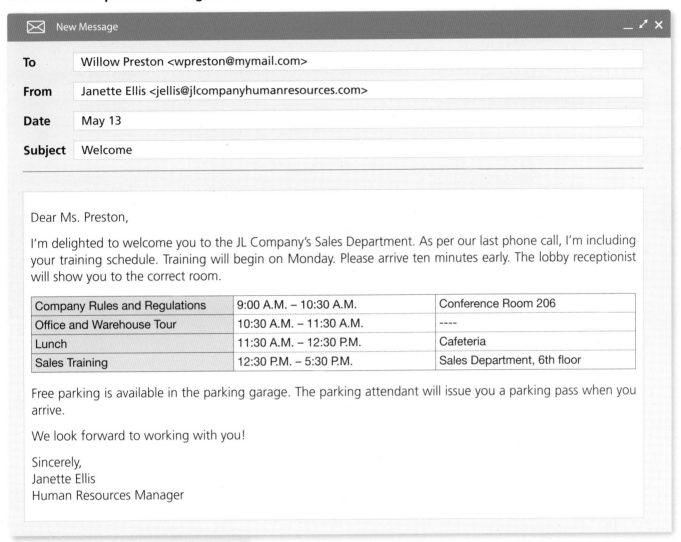

✉ New Message	_ ↗ ✕

To	Willow Preston <wpreston@mymail.com>
From	Janette Ellis <jellis@jlcompanyhumanresources.com>
Date	May 13
Subject	Welcome

Dear Ms. Preston,

I'm delighted to welcome you to the JL Company's Sales Department. As per our last phone call, I'm including your training schedule. Training will begin on Monday. Please arrive ten minutes early. The lobby receptionist will show you to the correct room.

Company Rules and Regulations	9:00 A.M. – 10:30 A.M.	Conference Room 206
Office and Warehouse Tour	10:30 A.M. – 11:30 A.M.	----
Lunch	11:30 A.M. – 12:30 P.M.	Cafeteria
Sales Training	12:30 P.M. – 5:30 P.M.	Sales Department, 6th floor

Free parking is available in the parking garage. The parking attendant will issue you a parking pass when you arrive.

We look forward to working with you!

Sincerely,
Janette Ellis
Human Resources Manager

Business English Dos and Don'ts

When welcoming new recruits to a company, there are some important things to remember. Be brief and specific when relaying information.

Dos	**Don'ts**
○ Training will begin on Monday. (*brief*)	✕ You'll have to start training next week in the morning. (*not specific*)
○ Please arrive ten minutes early. (*brief*)	✕ You should get here a bit early just in case. (*not specific*)

Explain procedures in a clear manner. Avoid being vague when giving information.

Dos	**Don'ts**
○ The lobby receptionist will show you to the correct room. (*clear*)	✕ There should be someone in the lobby to guide you. (*vague*)
○ The parking attendant will issue you a parking pass. (*clear*)	✕ All new employees need parking passes. (*vague*)

Situation ①

A Sam Park messages his coworkers to plan an orientation session. Read the instant message chain.

11:20 A.M. Hi, all! We've just finished our spring hiring period. It's time to plan the orientation session. — Sam Park

Henry Reed: I think May 1 or 2 would be best. **11:22 A.M.**

11:23 A.M. May 2 works. Henry, will you give the opening speech at 9:30 A.M.? — Sam Park

Henry Reed: Sure. No problem. **11:25 A.M.**

11:27 A.M. Rosa, can Mr. Winters deliver the CEO speech at 10:00 A.M.? — Sam Park

Rosa Green: I've just checked Mr. Winters' schedule. He'll be out of town during the first week of May. **11:30 A.M.**

11:32 A.M. Oh, I see. What if we delayed the orientation? — Sam Park

Rosa Green: He'll be back in the office on May 9. **11:35 A.M.**

11:37 A.M. Okay. May 9 it is. — Sam Park

Bonnie Hunt: Mr. Park, would you like me to lead the lab tour again this year? **11:40 A.M.**

11:44 A.M. Yes, from 10:30 to 12:00 P.M. Then, we'll serve lunch in the cafeteria for an hour. — Sam Park

Bonnie Hunt: I'll call the caterer about that. **11:46 A.M.**

11:48 A.M. Thanks, Bonnie. Following lunch, the trainees will go to their departments for more training. — Sam Park

Henry Reed: I'll send an email to the department managers. They need to prepare ID cards and security passcodes in advance. **11:52 A.M.**

Pop-up Questions

1 What did the company recently finish?
2 What will Mr. Reed do at 9:30 A.M.?
3 When will the orientation session happen?
4 Who will Ms. Hunt call?

B Take Notes :: Based on the instant message chain in A, complete the schedule.

Georgina Labs Orientation Session	Date: May 9
9:30 A.M. – 10:00 A.M.	1_____ Speech (delivered by Henry Reed)
10:00 A.M. – 10:30 A.M.	2_____ Speech (delivered by Mr. Winters)
10:30 A.M. – 12:00 P.M.	3_____ of the Labs (conducted by Bonnie Hunt)
12:00 P.M. – 1:00 P.M.	Catered Lunch in the 4_____ (arranged by Bonnie Hunt)
1:00 P.M. – 5:00 P.M.	Department-Specific Training (conducted by 5_____)

Background Knowledge

A Read and learn about orientation sessions.

Most new employees are not familiar with the company's rules and regulations. They also have many questions about their job duties. Thus, companies usually provide an orientation session. Orientation sessions benefit new employees in a few ways.

Firstly, an orientation session provides new employees with a general welcome to the company. The company's CEO might give a speech. This speech often details the history and the culture of the company. New employees learn more about the company's environment and mission.

Secondly, a good orientation session will take new employees on a tour. Whether there are warehouses, labs, or offices, employees get a chance to see where everything is located. Finally, most orientation sessions include department-specific training. New employees head to their respective departments to learn more about their jobs. Department managers might issue ID cards, security passcodes, and parking passes at this time.

Pop-up Questions

1 What does the CEO's speech often detail?
2 Why do new employees head to their respective departments?

B Listen to the talk and answer the questions. 02-1

1 Who is Priya Tasmir?
  a. a caterer   b. a manager   c. a security guard

2 What will the employees do in the lab?
  a. watch a demonstration   b. listen to a speech   c. make ID cards

3 What is NOT something the employees need?
  a. a passcode   b. an ID card   c. safety shoes

Vocabulary

A Learn some words related to orientation sessions.

People

 HR employee
 IT consultant
 trainer
 security specialist
 CEO / upper-level executive
 guide

*HR: Human Resources
*IT: Information Technology

Activities

 introduce oneself / meet colleagues

 fill out forms / sign documents

 receive an ID card

 watch a training video

 take a tour

 listen to one's speech

B Complete the sentences with the words in the box.

trainer	introduce myself	CEO	listen to his speech
guide	take a tour	watch a training video	receive an ID card

1 The _____ and founder of the company will say a few words now.

2 Please say hello to Ryan, who will be your _____ during the tour.

3 After lunch, we will _____ of the warehouses.

4 Please go to room 122 to _____. You need it to enter the building each day.

5 I am your _____ for the afternoon. I'll teach you all about the Sales Department.

6 Let me take a moment to _____. I'm Becky from the Human Resources Department.

7 To start, we're going to hear from Mr. Knight. Let's _____.

8 You're going to _____ in your department after the tour.

Speak Up

Practice the conversation with your partner by using the information in each schedule. 🔊 02-2

Example

Brice Shipping Orientation Session Date: September 4	
9:00 A.M. – 10:00 A.M.	Welcome Speech (delivered by Barry Root)
10:00 A.M. – 11:30 A.M.	Training Videos
11:30 A.M. – 12:00 P.M.	Question-and-Answer Session (conducted by Jenna Bloor)
12:00 P.M. – 1:00 P.M.	Catered Lunch in Conference Room 2 (arranged by Joshua McDonald)
1:00 P.M. – 2:00 P.M.	Warehouse Tour (conducted by Sylvia Prince)

Schedule 1

Ridge University Staff Orientation Session Date: January 10	
10:00 A.M. – 10:30 A.M.	Welcome Speech (delivered by Dean Eaton)
10:30 A.M. – 11:30 A.M.	Department-Specific Training (conducted by department managers)
11:30 A.M. – 12:30 P.M.	Question-and-Answer Session (conducted by Barry Root)
12:30 P.M. – 1:30 P.M.	Catered Lunch in the West Cafeteria (arranged by Sylvia Prince)
1:30 P.M. – 4:00 P.M.	Campus Tour (conducted by Jenna Bloor)

Schedule 2

Edge Technologies Orientation Session Date: May 17	
10:00 A.M. – 10:30 A.M.	CEO Speech (delivered by Barrett White)
10:30 A.M. – 12:30 P.M.	Warehouse and Office Tours (conducted by Barry Root)
12:30 P.M. – 1:30 P.M.	Lunch at Holly's Buffet (arranged by Sylvia Prince)
1:30 P.M. – 2:30 P.M.	Question-and-Answer Session (conducted by Jenna Bloor)
2:30 P.M. – 5:30 P.M.	Department-Specific Training (conducted by department managers)

A Hey, Barry. Do you know when the orientation session is?

B Hi, Jenna. Here. I just made this schedule.

A Thanks. So it's on September 4.

B You're doing the question-and-answer session this year.

A Right. I thought so. I did it last year, too.

B I remember. You did a great job.

A It looks like you're doing the welcome speech.

B Yeah. I'm a bit nervous about it.

A You'll do fine. Does Sylvia know she's conducting the warehouse tour?

B Not yet. I'm going to tell her today.

Tips for Success

When planning an orientation session, ensure that all employees understand their duties prior to the orientation day.

19

A **Let's learn about the uses of *do*.**

Do as a main verb means "to carry out an action."	*Do* as a helping verb is used to ask questions.
You'll **do** fine on the test.	**Do** you know when the meeting is?
He **did** a great job during his presentation.	**Does** Janet know she has a meeting?
You're **doing** the question-and-answer session tomorrow.	**Did** he leave the conference early?
Mr. Chang **does** all of the hiring in February.	**Do** they leave work around 5:00 P.M.?

B **Complete the following sentences with the correct form of *do*.**

1 You're _____ the welcome speech this time.

2 _____ Steve know Mr. Wallace just called?

3 You'll _____ a great job tomorrow.

4 _____ you go to the expo last year?

5 _____ Sandra and Max work in Sales now?

6 Emma _____ research for a company in Spain these days.

7 _____ they apply for the job already?

8 Tom, you're _____ the interviews this year.

📶 Know-how *at* Work   **How to Plan an Orientation**

Before employees begin working, they should attend an orientation session. The session will familiarize them with the company. Those in charge of planning the session should make a schedule in advance.

1 Make a list of who will be involved in the orientation session. Some employees leave the office regularly or travel on business. Choose a day that is convenient for everyone involved.

2 Ask the trainees to gather in one place when they arrive. Schedule speeches during this time. This can provide the trainees with general information about the company.

3 Plan to have a lunch break that is an hour or longer. This will allow trainees to get to know one another as well as their managers.

4 Finish the orientation session with department-specific training. Send trainees to their respective departments to meet their managers, to get familiar with their workstations, and to learn more about their job duties.

5 If necessary, schedule a tour of the facilities. In addition, make sure there's time to fill out paperwork, to receive ID cards, and to watch safety demonstrations.

Situation ❷

Ⓐ Sam Park gets a call from Rosa Green about the orientation session. Read the voicemail message.

◀🔊 02-3

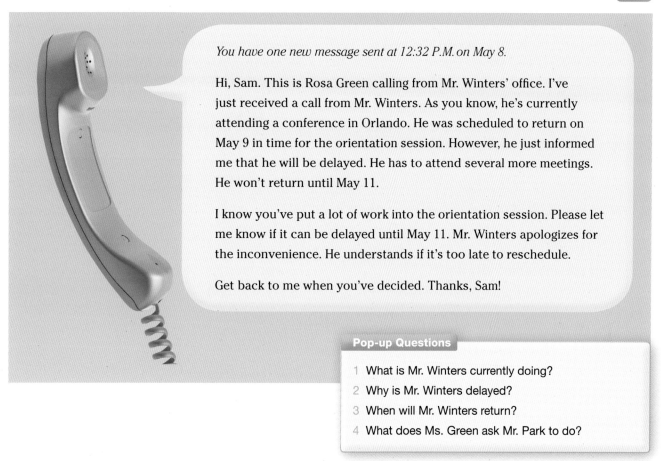

You have one new message sent at 12:32 P.M. on May 8.

Hi, Sam. This is Rosa Green calling from Mr. Winters' office. I've just received a call from Mr. Winters. As you know, he's currently attending a conference in Orlando. He was scheduled to return on May 9 in time for the orientation session. However, he just informed me that he will be delayed. He has to attend several more meetings. He won't return until May 11.

I know you've put a lot of work into the orientation session. Please let me know if it can be delayed until May 11. Mr. Winters apologizes for the inconvenience. He understands if it's too late to reschedule.

Get back to me when you've decided. Thanks, Sam!

Pop-up Questions

1 What is Mr. Winters currently doing?
2 Why is Mr. Winters delayed?
3 When will Mr. Winters return?
4 What does Ms. Green ask Mr. Park to do?

Ⓑ Problem Solving :: Sam Park must call Bonnie Hunt to ask if the lab tour can be postponed until May 11. Find a partner and choose the roles of Sam Park and Bonnie Hunt. Then, role-play to discuss a possible solution. Use the information from situations 1 and 2 if necessary.

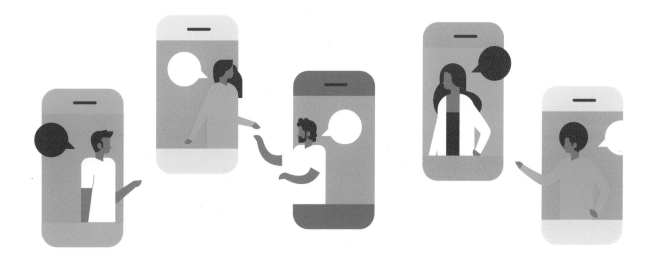

 **Useful Expressions**

A Let's learn some expressions to use in business.

When acknowledging someone's efforts	When acknowledging your team's efforts
I know you've put a lot of work into the orientation session. I understand your team has worked hard this year. I appreciate your help with the matter.	We've put a lot of work into the training session. We worked very hard to complete the project in time. My team has done a great job planning the company party.
When referencing prior information	**When making a compromise**
As you know, he's currently attending a conference. As you're aware, the company picnic was canceled. As you've heard, we will move to a new office soon.	He understands if it's too late to reschedule. It's all right if we need to delay the launch. It is fine if the delivery is a little late.

B Fill in the blanks with the correct answers from the box. Then, practice the conversation with a partner. 🔊 02-4

my team worked very hard	I understand you've put a lot of effort into
understands if it's too late to reschedule	as you're aware

A Hi, Walter. This is Rita calling from Mr. Hong's office.

B Hi, Rita. What can I help you with?

A ¹_____, Mr. Hong is currently overseas.

B Yes, I heard that.

A His flight was delayed, so he won't return in time for the orientation session.

B Oh, that's a problem.

A ²_____ planning the orientation.

B Yes, ³_____.

A Is it too late to postpone it?

B I think so. We've already booked the caterer and the warehouse tour.

A That's all right. Mr. Hong ⁴_____.

Extra Practice

Role-play with your partner. One person asks if an event can be rescheduled. The other person denies the request.

A I know you've put a lot of work into the training session.

B Yes, my team worked very hard to plan it.

A Is it possible to reschedule it? Ms. Trent understands if it's too late.

B No, I don't think it's possible.

Situation 3

Sam Park gives a speech during the orientation session. Read the talk and see if the results are positive or negative. 🔊 02-5

Thanks for starting us off, Henry.

Hello, everyone. My name is Sam Park. I'm the Human Resources manager here at Georgina Labs. I'd like to take this opportunity to congratulate you all. I hope you enjoy your time working here.

Before we start, I have to mention something. Normally, our CEO, Mr. Bob Winters, delivers this speech. He regrets that he can't be here today. He's currently traveling on business. However, he's looking forward to meeting you all when he returns.

Instead of Mr. Winters' speech, you're going to see a short video. The video will give you a brief history of Georgina Labs. It will include a message from our founder, the late Georgina Harper. Additionally, you'll get an introduction to some of our most popular products.

Following that, we'll begin the lab tour. Are there any questions?

Business English Dos and Don'ts

When expressing regret on behalf of a manager or CEO, there are a few things to consider. Be specific about what the manager or CEO wishes to express.

Dos	Don'ts
○ He regrets that he can't be here today. (*specific*)	✗ He must feel bad about it, but I'm not sure. (*vague*)
○ He's looking forward to meeting you all when he returns. (*specific*)	✗ I'm sure you'll meet him at some point in the future. (*vague*)

Briefly mention why the manager or CEO wishes to express regret.

Dos	Don'ts
○ He's currently traveling on business. (*reason*)	✗ He can't be here. (*no reason*)
○ She's out of town and won't return in time for the event. (*reason*)	✗ She won't attend the event. (*no reason*)

Situation ❶

Ⓐ **Regina Weston asks Eric Hunt to conduct a customer satisfaction survey. Read the telephone conversation.** 🔊 03-1

🕾 **Regina Weston** Hi, Eric. I'm sure you're aware that we had a drop in sales this quarter.

🕾 **Eric Hunt** Yes, I heard. That's very disappointing.

🕾 **Regina Weston** I think it would be best if we got some customer feedback. That way, we can work on attracting new customers.

🕾 **Eric Hunt** What do you suggest?

🕾 **Regina Weston** I'd like you to put together a customer satisfaction survey.

🕾 **Eric Hunt** Sure. What should I include in the survey?

🕾 **Regina Weston** Since we specialize in delivering prepackaged meals, I'd like to get some feedback on those products. We should ask about the overall quality.

🕾 **Eric Hunt** Okay. And how about the delivery service?

🕾 **Regina Weston** Yes, I'd like to get some feedback about packaging, too. We should also ask about delivery speed.

🕾 **Eric Hunt** Great. Anything else?

🕾 **Regina Weston** Yes, we just launched an app. Customers can place orders that way. I'm curious if the app is easy to use or if they prefer the website.

🕾 **Eric Hunt** All right. I'll add a section about that.

🕾 **Regina Weston** Let's also include a section about our customer service hotline. I'd like to know how easy it is to return damaged items.

Pop-up Questions

1. What does Ms. Weston want to attract?
2. What does Ms. Weston ask Mr. Hunt to do?
3. What does the company specialize in?
4. What did the company recently launch?

B Take Notes :: Based on the conversation in A, complete the memo.

- Create a customer [1] _____ survey - will be completed by Eric Hunt

- Include:

  a. Products - overall [2] _____

  b. Feedback about [3] _____

  c. Delivery [4] _____

  d. App - easy to use or customers prefer the [5] _____

  e. Customer [6] _____ - how easy is it to return [7] _____ items

Background Knowledge

A Read and learn about ways to conduct surveys.

It is important for businesses to collect opinions from customers. This can be done by conducting a customer satisfaction survey. During a survey, customers can provide honest feedback about a company's goods and services. This helps companies change or develop new policies.

There are several ways to conduct a customer satisfaction survey. Traditionally, companies conducted in-person surveys. However, these can be costly and time consuming. Telephone surveys later became more common. Company representatives call customers and ask a series of questions. Unfortunately, many customers do not feel comfortable sharing information over the phone.

As a result, online surveys are now the most widely used method. Online surveys are fast and effective. Businesses can ask complex questions and get quick feedback. Customers can complete the surveys on their computers or smartphones. Thus, the response rate is very high compared to other survey methods.

Pop-up Questions

1 What do surveys help companies do?

2 What is the most widely used survey method?

B Listen to the conversation and answer the questions. 🔊 03-2

1 Who will make the survey?

a. Katherine   b. Melinda   c. Arthur

2 What will the survey NOT ask about?

a. customer service   b. packaging   c. refund policies

3 When will the survey launch?

a. at the end of the year   b. next Friday   c. in two weeks

Vocabulary

A **Learn some survey topics.**

	Survey Topic	Definition
1	product/service quality	the overall condition of a product or a service
2	product/service pricing	the price of a product or a service
3	product warranty	an agreement to fix or replace a product for a set period of time
4	customer service	support offered to customers prior to, during, and after purchasing a product or a service
5	refund/exchange policy	a promise to return payment or to provide a replacement if a product or service is unsatisfactory
6	delivery speed	how fast or slow a product reaches a customer
7	packaging	the boxes, bubble wrap, and other materials used to protect products during shipping
8	billing accuracy	the correctness of the amount customers are asked to pay

B **Read each customer complaint and write the correct survey topic in the blank.**

1

There was an issue with my most recent delivery. The boxes were badly dented. There also wasn't enough bubble wrap inside. As a result, some of the items were damaged. Two of the glasses were broken in half.

2

When I checked my credit card statement this month, I noticed I was charged twice for an order. The amount $134.00 appears twice, first on October 3 and again on October 5. However, I only placed one order that month.

3

I called the hotline on September 18. The representative I spoke to was extremely rude. He refused to listen to the problems I had with my order. Then, he refused to let me discuss it with a manager. I don't plan to order from you again.

4

I placed an order on July 24. The website noted that it would arrive within 2 to 3 business days. However, a week passed, and my order didn't arrive. Customer service promised to solve the problem, but I still didn't receive the order for another two weeks.

Speak Up

Practice the conversation with your partner by using the information in each memo. ◀) 03-3

Example

Create a customer satisfaction survey

– will be completed by Pierre

Include:

a. Product quality

b. Product pricing

c. Our customer service

d. Refund policy – easy to get a refund

Memo 1

Create a customer satisfaction survey

– will be completed by Renaldo

Include:

a. Delivery speed

b. Packaging

c. Our website

d. Customer service hotline – easy to return damaged items

Memo 2

Create a customer satisfaction survey

– will be completed by Minji

Include:

a. Service quality

b. Service pricing

c. Our marketing

d. App – simple and easy to use

Memo 3

Create a customer satisfaction survey

– will be completed by Hannah

Include:

a. Product warranty

b. Billing accuracy

c. Customer loyalty

d. Exchange policy – fair and helpful

A Hi, Pierre. I'd like you to put together a customer satisfaction survey.

B Sure. What should I include in the survey?

A First, I'd like to get some feedback on product quality.

B Okay. What else?

A I'm curious how our customers feel about our product pricing, too.

B Understood. How about customer service?

A Yes, please include a section about customer service.

B Will do. Is that all?

A No, we should also ask about our refund policy.

   I want to know if it's easy to get a refund.

B Good idea. I'll start on the survey right away.

! Tips for Success

When developing a survey, try to include a variety of topics in order to best understand each customer's experience.

 **GRAMMAR**

A Let's learn about direct and indirect questions.

Direct Question	Indirect Question
How do our customers feel about our product pricing? Where are they going to hold the meeting? What is the total cost of the order?	Can you tell me how our customers feel about our product pricing? Do you know where they are going to hold the meeting? Could you let me know what the total cost of the order is?
Indirect Question in a Statement	
I'm curious how our customers feel about our product pricing. I want to know where they are going to hold the meeting. I'd like to know what the total cost of the order is.	

B Complete the following sentences by changing each direct question to an indirect question.

1 Why was he fired from his last job? → I want to know _____.

2 Where can I submit my application form? → Can you tell me _____?

3 When is the company picnic? → Could you let me know _____?

4 What is the company's policy? → I'm curious _____.

5 How was the orientation session? → Do you know _____?

6 Where is the new office? → I wonder _____.

7 What is the application deadline? → Would you mind telling me _____?

8 Why was he upset this afternoon? → Do you mind me asking _____?

Know-how *at* Work   **How to Conduct an Online Survey**

Online surveys are one of the best ways to collect customer opinions. These surveys are quick and easy and allow businesses to get feedback from a large number of customers.

1 There are many online survey platforms. Some are free while others require a membership fee. Some platforms limit the number of responses, so choose the one that best suits your company's needs.

2 Upload your questions and then launch your survey. Reach out to your customers by email. If customers are reluctant to reply, offer a discount coupon in exchange for their cooperation.

3 Once you have enough data, it's time to analyze it. Look at patterns in the information. Find areas of weakness and brainstorm possible solutions.

4 Finally, write a report about your survey. Highlight what customers liked best. Explain weaknesses and then suggest several possible solutions. This will help your company improve customer satisfaction.

Situation 2

A Regina Weston gets a link to the survey she asked Eric Hunt to create. Read the survey.

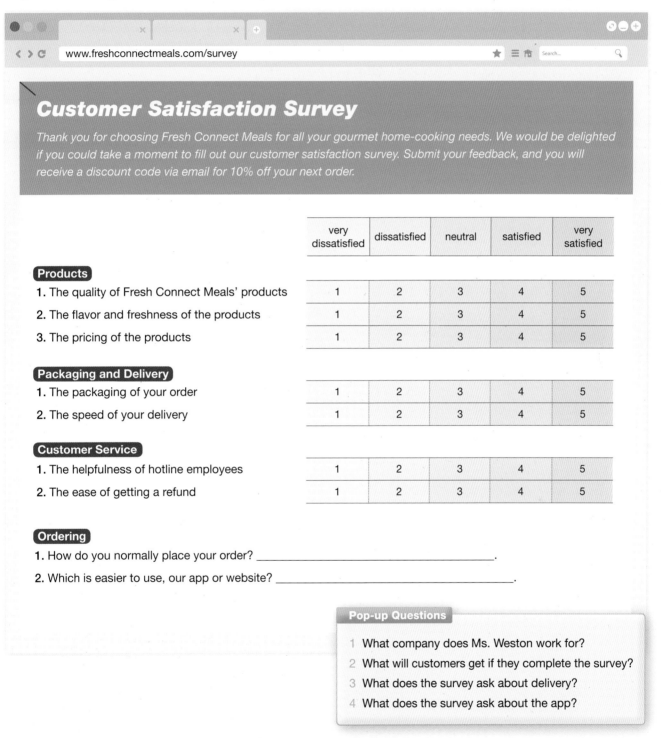

www.freshconnectmeals.com/survey

Customer Satisfaction Survey

Thank you for choosing Fresh Connect Meals for all your gourmet home-cooking needs. We would be delighted if you could take a moment to fill out our customer satisfaction survey. Submit your feedback, and you will receive a discount code via email for 10% off your next order.

	very dissatisfied	dissatisfied	neutral	satisfied	very satisfied
Products					
1. The quality of Fresh Connect Meals' products	1	2	3	4	5
2. The flavor and freshness of the products	1	2	3	4	5
3. The pricing of the products	1	2	3	4	5
Packaging and Delivery					
1. The packaging of your order	1	2	3	4	5
2. The speed of your delivery	1	2	3	4	5
Customer Service					
1. The helpfulness of hotline employees	1	2	3	4	5
2. The ease of getting a refund	1	2	3	4	5

Ordering

1. How do you normally place your order? _____.

2. Which is easier to use, our app or website? _____.

Pop-up Questions

1 What company does Ms. Weston work for?

2 What will customers get if they complete the survey?

3 What does the survey ask about delivery?

4 What does the survey ask about the app?

B **Problem Solving ::** Regina Weston calls Eric Hunt to ask him to add an additional feedback question to the survey. Find a partner and choose the roles of Regina Weston and Eric Hunt. Then, role-play to discuss a possible solution. Use the information from the survey in A if necessary.

A Let's learn some expressions to use in business.

When expressing gratitude with a request	When providing an incentive with instructions
We would be delighted if you could fill out our survey. We would be grateful if you provided some feedback. I would appreciate your help with this situation. Thank you in advance for your assistance.	Submit your feedback, and you will receive a discount. Fill out this survey, and you will receive a free gift. Add your phone number, and you'll get a coupon. Enter your email address, and you could win the grand prize.
When asking about frequency	When asking about a preference
How do you normally place your order? Where do you usually buy your groceries? How often do you shop online?	Which is easier to use, our app or website? How do you prefer to shop, online or in the store? Which benefit is better, free shipping or a discount?

B Fill in the blanks with the correct answers from the box. Then, practice the conversation with a partner. ◁» 03-4

which is easier to use, our app or website	go to our website
how often do you shop at	I would be grateful if you provided

A Hello, Mr. Chong. This is Veronica from Amhurst Online Market.

B Oh, hello.

A Mr. Chong, we're conducting a customer satisfaction survey.
   ¹_____ some feedback.

B Sure, that's fine.

A Great. First, ²_____ Amhurst Online Market?

B Usually, about 2 or 3 times per month.

A I see. And ³_____?

B Well, I used to prefer the app. But after the last update, it often freezes.

A Thank you for your feedback. I'd like to invite you to fill out a more detailed survey.

B Maybe if I have time.

A ⁴_____, and you will receive a discount on your next order.

Extra Practice

Role-play with your partner. One person asks for feedback, and the other provides it.

A Hello. I would grateful if you provided some feedback.

B Sure, that's fine.

A How do you prefer to shop, online or in the store?

B I used to prefer online. But the website often freezes now.

Situation 3

Regina Weston emails Eric Hunt about the survey he conducted. Read the email and see if the results are positive or negative.

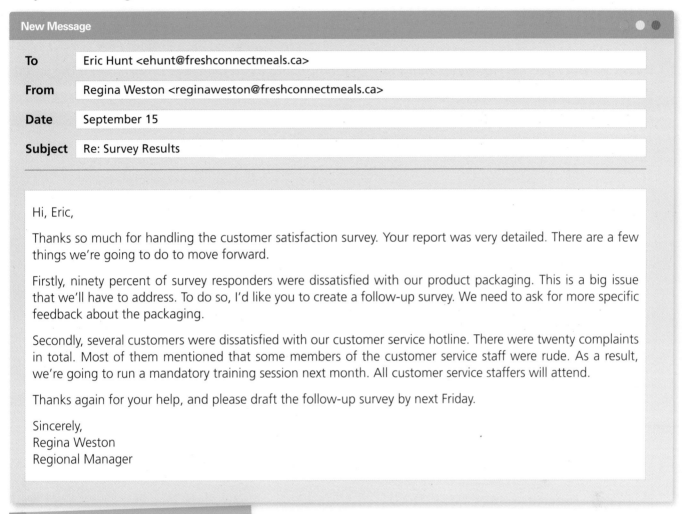

New Message

To	Eric Hunt <ehunt@freshconnectmeals.ca>
From	Regina Weston <reginaweston@freshconnectmeals.ca>
Date	September 15
Subject	Re: Survey Results

Hi, Eric,

Thanks so much for handling the customer satisfaction survey. Your report was very detailed. There are a few things we're going to do to move forward.

Firstly, ninety percent of survey responders were dissatisfied with our product packaging. This is a big issue that we'll have to address. To do so, I'd like you to create a follow-up survey. We need to ask for more specific feedback about the packaging.

Secondly, several customers were dissatisfied with our customer service hotline. There were twenty complaints in total. Most of them mentioned that some members of the customer service staff were rude. As a result, we're going to run a mandatory training session next month. All customer service staffers will attend.

Thanks again for your help, and please draft the follow-up survey by next Friday.

Sincerely,
Regina Weston
Regional Manager

Business English Dos and Don'ts

When discussing survey data, there are a few important things to remember. Use numbers and percentages to back up your observations.

Dos
- Ninety percent of responders were dissatisfied with our packaging. (*numerical*)
- There were twenty complaints in total. (*numerical*)

Don'ts
- ✗ The majority of responders weren't happy with our packaging. (*not specific enough*)
- ✗ I think we had several complaints. (*not specific enough*)

Relay data and trends in a neutral way. Avoid overly emotional phrases.

Dos
- This is a big issue that we'll have to address. (*neutral*)
- Most of them mentioned the customer service staff was rude. (*neutral*)

Don'ts
- ✗ This is a disaster! (*too emotional*)
- ✗ I can't believe we employ so many rude people. (*too emotional*)

Situation ①

A David Stewart gets an email informing him of job opening at an overseas branch. Read the email.

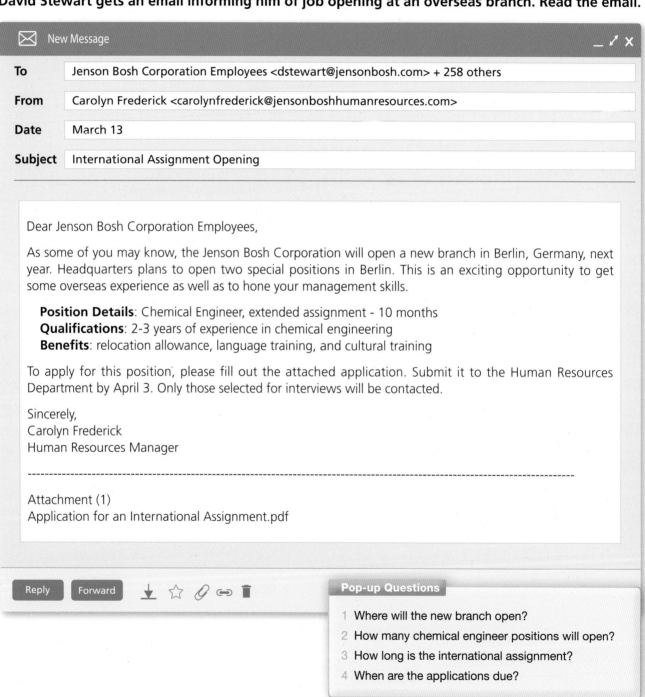

✉	New Message	_ ⤢ ✕

To	Jenson Bosh Corporation Employees <dstewart@jensonbosh.com> + 258 others
From	Carolyn Frederick <carolynfrederick@jensonboshhumanresources.com>
Date	March 13
Subject	International Assignment Opening

Dear Jenson Bosh Corporation Employees,

As some of you may know, the Jenson Bosh Corporation will open a new branch in Berlin, Germany, next year. Headquarters plans to open two special positions in Berlin. This is an exciting opportunity to get some overseas experience as well as to hone your management skills.

Position Details: Chemical Engineer, extended assignment - 10 months
Qualifications: 2-3 years of experience in chemical engineering
Benefits: relocation allowance, language training, and cultural training

To apply for this position, please fill out the attached application. Submit it to the Human Resources Department by April 3. Only those selected for interviews will be contacted.

Sincerely,
Carolyn Frederick
Human Resources Manager

Attachment (1)
Application for an International Assignment.pdf

Reply Forward ↓ ☆ 𝄾 ⇔ 🗑

Pop-up Questions

1 Where will the new branch open?

2 How many chemical engineer positions will open?

3 How long is the international assignment?

4 When are the applications due?

B Take Notes :: Based on the email in A, complete the job posting.

Job: International Assignment

Open To: all Jenson Bosh Corporation employees

Purpose: to get some overseas experience and to hone your management skills

Location: [1] ----------------------------

Applications Due: [2] ----------------------------

Position: [3] ---------------------- (two positions)

Send To: Carolyn Frederick in [4] ----------------------------

Duration: [5] ---------------------- months

Qualifications: 2-3 years of experience in chemical engineering

Benefits: relocation allowance, [6] ----------------------, and cultural training

Background Knowledge

A Read and learn about international assignments.

Many businesses have overseas branches or partner companies. Sometimes employees travel overseas to work at a partner branch. This is called an international assignment. There are three types of international assignments. Short-term assignments last for six months or fewer. Extended assignments may last for up to a year. Traditional long-term assignments range from twelve months to three years.

Employees who go on international assignments are called expatriates. Expatriates benefit from international assignments in many ways. They can gain experience in technical or management positions. They can also improve their organizational skills. Finally, their understanding of overseas business practices will improve.

International assignments are not easy, however. Moving to a new country is challenging. This is especially true for employees with families. Many people experience culture shock in a new country. Employees should learn about the country and its culture before going on an international assignment.

Pop-up Questions

1 How many types of international assignments are there?

2 What should employees learn about before an international assignment?

B Listen to the conversation and answer the questions. ◀) 04-1

1 **What are the man and the woman discussing?**

a. a job in Paris   b. a culture class   c. an office in Russia

2 **Who will apply for the international assignment?**

a. Karen   b. Rob   c. Marina

3 **What aspect of the job is the woman worried about?**

a. the workload   b. the expenses   c. the length

Vocabulary

A Learn some words related to international assignments.

	Word	Definition
1	application	a form used to make a request or to apply for a job
2	interview	a meeting to determine if a candidate is qualified for a job
3	cultural training	classes that help employees understand an unfamiliar culture
4	relocation allowance	funds given to an employee to help with the cost of relocating
5	culture shock	a state of discomfort when one is immersed in an unfamiliar culture
6	language barrier	the inability to communicate with someone in that person's language
7	homesickness	a feeling of sadness or longing for one's home
8	management skills	the abilities and the methods of a manager
9	overseas experience	work experience gathered in a foreign country
10	expatriate	a person who resides and works in a foreign country

B Read the sentences on the left and match them with the correct words on the right.

1 I'm going to submit a(n) _____ for the job in Moscow.   •   • a. cultural training

2 She suffered from _____ during her stay in China.   •   • b. application

3 He's a(n) _____ who has worked overseas for 5 years.   •   • c. homesickness

4 I have a(n) _____ with the Human Resources manager at 2:00 P.M.   •   • d. management skills

5 The company provides a(n) _____ to help with the cost of moving.   •   • e. language barrier

6 My family and I will take some _____ classes before relocating.   •   • f. relocation allowance

7 I only speak English, so the _____ is a problem.   •   • g. interview

8 He's hoping to improve his _____ during the assignment.   •   • h. expatriate

Speak Up

Practice the conversation with your partner by using the information in each job posting. 04-2

(Example)

Job Location: Paris, France
Position: Financial Analyst
Duration: 18 months
Qualifications: 3-4 years of experience in finance
Benefits: a relocation allowance

Applications Due: August 24
Send To: Jerald Meyers in Human Resources

(Posting 1)

Job Location: Mendoza, Argentina
Position: Urban Planner
Duration: 2-3 years
Qualifications: 5-6 years of experience in urban planning at the management level
Benefits: language training

Applications Due: November 10
Send To: Walter Briggs in Human Resources

(Posting 2)

Job Location: Cairo, Egypt
Position: Curator
Duration: 1-2 years
Qualifications: 5-7 years of experience as a museum curator
Benefits: cultural training

Applications Due: January 3
Send To: Paul Wilson in Human Resources

(Posting 3)

Job Location: Beijing, China
Position: Aerospace Engineer
Duration: 2-3 years
Qualifications: 2-3 years of experience in aerospace engineering
Benefits: a relocation allowance

Applications Due: March 3
Send To: Margo Fields in Human Resources

A Hi, Gina. Did you get the email from Human Resources?

B About the international assignments? Yeah, I did.

A I'm thinking of applying for the financial analyst position.

B Oh, that would be great for you.

A Yeah, it's 18 months long in Paris, France.

B How much experience do you need to apply?

A At least 3-4 years of experience in finance.

B I see. You should definitely apply.

A I think I will. The company even provides a relocation allowance.

B Make sure to send your application to Jerald by August 24.

! Tips for Success

When looking at job postings, check if the company provides successful candidates with any special benefits.

A Let's learn about quantifiers.

Countable	Uncountable
Use *a few* and *many* to describe the amount of a countable noun.	Use *a little* and *much* to describe the amount of an uncountable noun.
There are **a few** applications to submit. He worked there for **many** years.	There is **a little** ink in the cartridge. Unfortunately, I don't have **much** experience.
Use *lots of* and *some* for both countable and uncountable nouns.	
There are **lots of/a lot of** chairs in the conference room. He delivered **some** boxes to the lobby.	There is **lots of/a lot of** paper in the copy machine. She spilled **some** coffee onto the forms.

B Correct the mistake in the underlined part of each sentence.

1 We have a <u>fews</u> problems to discuss before we conclude the meeting.

2 He delivered some <u>box</u> to the lobby on the first floor.

3 Unfortunately, she doesn't have <u>many</u> experience as an accountant.

4 There is only <u>much</u> coffee left. We don't have enough for everyone.

5 He put <u>many</u> ink into the printer last night.

6 They have attended <u>much</u> conferences over the years.

7 Let's move some <u>chair</u> into the breakroom before lunch.

8 He will take <u>somes</u> of her clients while she is away.

Know-how *at* **Work**   How to Be Successful during an Interview

Interviews are an important part of the job-selection process. If you want a company to hire you, you must perform well during the interview. There are a few things to remember.

1 You might be nervous in an interview, so prepare for the interview in advance. Ask a friend or colleague to do a mock interview with you. You can also practice in front of a mirror.

2 During the interview, speak clearly and confidently. Try to make eye contact and smile. Be friendly and relaxed but not too casual. You should be as professional as possible.

3 When answering questions, don't spend too much time thinking about your answers. Try to answer quickly and honestly. Talk about your work experience in a positive manner.

4 Highlight your achievements and skills. Make sure the interviewer knows why you want the job and what you can do for the company. When the interview is over, thank the interviewer for his or her time.

Situation 2

A David Stewart gets an email from Carolyn Frederick informing him that he passed the application stage. Read the email.

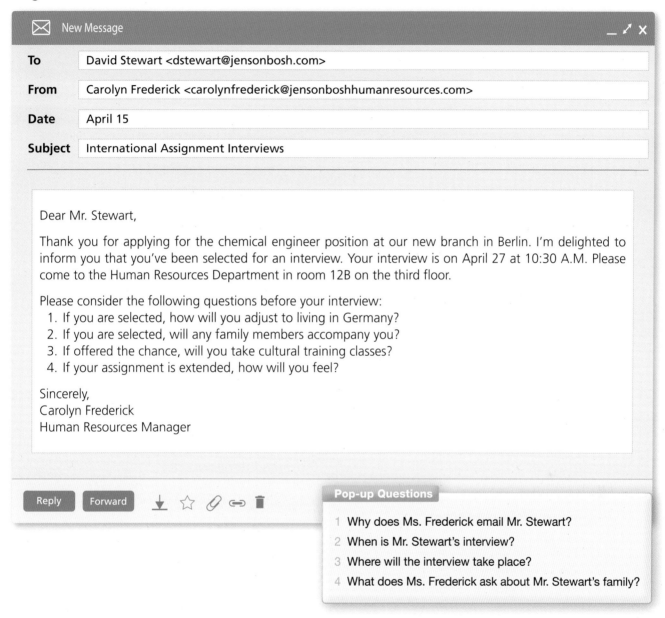

✉ New Message ⎯ ↗ ✕

To	David Stewart <dstewart@jensonbosh.com>
From	Carolyn Frederick <carolynfrederick@jensonboshhumanresources.com>
Date	April 15
Subject	International Assignment Interviews

Dear Mr. Stewart,

Thank you for applying for the chemical engineer position at our new branch in Berlin. I'm delighted to inform you that you've been selected for an interview. Your interview is on April 27 at 10:30 A.M. Please come to the Human Resources Department in room 12B on the third floor.

Please consider the following questions before your interview:
1. If you are selected, how will you adjust to living in Germany?
2. If you are selected, will any family members accompany you?
3. If offered the chance, will you take cultural training classes?
4. If your assignment is extended, how will you feel?

Sincerely,
Carolyn Frederick
Human Resources Manager

Reply Forward ↓ ☆ 📎 🔗 🗑

Pop-up Questions

1 Why does Ms. Frederick email Mr. Stewart?
2 When is Mr. Stewart's interview?
3 Where will the interview take place?
4 What does Ms. Frederick ask about Mr. Stewart's family?

B **Problem Solving ::** David Stewart is unable to attend his interview on April 27. Find a partner and choose the roles of David Stewart and Carolyn Frederick. Then, role-play to discuss a possible solution. Use the information from the email in A if necessary.

A Let's learn some expressions to use in business.

When delivering good news	When responding to good news
I'm delighted to inform you that you've been selected for an interview. I'm pleased to offer you a position at our company. I'm happy to let you know that you were chosen for a promotion.	Thank you for informing me. That's wonderful to hear. What great news! I'm glad to hear it.
When informing someone of an appointment	**When providing further instructions**
Your interview is on April 27 at 10:30 A.M. The meeting will take place at 9:00 A.M. on Friday. Your appointment with Mr. Park is scheduled for March 3 at 3:00 P.M.	Please come to the Human Resources Department in room 12B on the third floor. Be in the auditorium by 8:00 A.M. Please arrive 15 minutes before the interview.

B Fill in the blanks with the correct answers from the box. Then, practice the conversation with a partner. 🔊 04-3

please come to the Human Resources Department	thank you for informing me
I'm happy to let you know that you were chosen	will take place at 10:00 A.M. on Monday

A Hello, Ms. Nakamura. This is Tom calling from Human Resources.

B Hello, Tom. How are you?

A Great, thanks. I'm calling about your application for the position in Barcelona.

B Oh, I see.

A ¹ _____ for an interview.

B That's wonderful to hear. ² _____.

A No problem. Your interview ³ _____.

B Okay. 10:00 A.M. on Monday. That's perfect.

A ⁴ _____ on the sixth floor.

B Sure. Sounds great. I'll see you then!

A Have a nice day, Ms. Nakamura.

Extra Practice

Role-play with your partner. One person informs an applicant of an interview time. The other person responds to the good news.

A I'm pleased to let you know that you were chosen for an interview.

B What great news!

A Please come to room 112 at 4:00 P.M. on June 3.

B Okay, great. See you then!

Situation 3

David Stewart sees a notice informing the employees of an employee transfer. Read the notice and see if the results are positive or negative.

Notice: Employee Transfer

Dear Jenson Bosh Corporation Staff,

I'm pleased to announce that David Stewart has been selected for the chemical engineer position in Berlin. David has worked for the Jenson Bosh Corporation for four years. Last year, he was promoted to assistant manager of his department.

Next month, David will depart for Berlin. He will spend 10 months there leading the chemical engineering team. This will be a great opportunity for him to gain experience in an overseas office. While David is away, Enrique Reyes and Yolanda Newton will take over David's duties. The Engineering Department will also bring on three new interns to assist.

Let's offer David Stewart our congratulations. Best wishes for an easy transition to life in Berlin!

Regards,
Carolyn Frederick
Human Resources Manager

Business English Dos and Don'ts

When writing an announcement, there are some important things to remember. Be specific and detailed. Present the information professionally.

Dos	Don'ts
○ Next month, David will depart for Berlin. (*specific*)	✕ David will head overseas for the job. (*vague*)
○ He will spend 10 months there leading the chemical engineering team. (*detailed*)	✕ He will work there for several months. (*vague*)

Anticipate questions that may arise. Try to answer them with specifics in the announcement.

Dos	Don'ts
○ Enrique Reyes and Yolanda Newton will take over David's duties. (*specific plan*)	✕ Some of you will have to cover David's duties. (*not specific*)
○ The Engineering Department will also bring on three new interns. (*specific plan*)	✕ We'll find others to help as well. (*not specific*)

Situation ❶

Ⓐ **Henrietta Cross of Everbridge Corp calls a coworker to ask him to help plan a charity event. Read the telephone conversation.** 🔊 05-1

☎ **Henrietta Cross** Hi, Benjamin. I just got a call from the CEO. He wants to host a charity event to benefit the local children's hospital.

☎ **Benjamin Morris** Thanks for letting me know, Ms. Cross. What type of event is it?

☎ **Henrietta Cross** The CEO prefers a live auction. Please ask Crystal to hire an auctioneer.

☎ **Benjamin Morris** Will do. Where should we hold the event?

☎ **Henrietta Cross** The Franklin Art Gallery often hosts events, so how about there? It will have to be in mid-March. I know the gallery gets booked fast though.

☎ **Benjamin Morris** I'll call today, but March is only two months away. That's not nearly enough time to plan everything.

☎ **Henrietta Cross** You're right. We'll just have to try our best.

☎ **Benjamin Morris** What sort of items will be auctioned?

☎ **Henrietta Cross** Paintings, sculptures— those sorts of things. We need to reach out to donors. I know Rick has connections in the local art community.

☎ **Benjamin Morris** Okay, I'll ask him. We should also set up an auction website. We can sell tickets there as well as advertise auction items.

☎ **Henrietta Cross** You can handle that. Please also let Derek know his team should arrange setup, catering, and cleanup.

☎ **Benjamin Morris** Sure. No problem!

Pop-up Questions

1 Who asked Ms. Cross to plan the event?
2 What type of event will take place?
3 When will the event take place?
4 Who will reach out to local donors?

B **Take Notes** :: Based on the telephone conversation in A, complete the memo.

Everbridge Corp - Memo

Event: a ¹_____ to benefit the local children's hospital   When: ²_____

Where: The Franklin ³_____

To Do:
Book the venue - Benjamin   Hire an ⁴_____ - Crystal
⁵_____ donors - Rick   ⁶_____ an auction website - Benjamin
Arrange setup, catering, and ⁷_____ - Derek and his team

Background Knowledge

A **Read and learn about how to plan a charity event.**

Charity fundraisers are a great way for businesses to give back to the community. When planning a fundraiser, first, pick a cause. You might want to help the environment, your city's veterans, or a local hospital. Choose the type of event you want to host. Auctions and sporting events are popular. Concerts and galas can also raise a lot of money.

Next, book a venue for your event. Art galleries, community centers, hotels, parks, and theaters are all great places to hold events. Make a list of equipment you need to rent. You might also need to arrange for catering or hire bartenders. If your company can afford it, hire an event planner to handle these details.

Finally, set a budget. Figure out how much your event will cost. Donations should cover the cost of your event plus an additional 30%. These funds will go directly to the charity. Advertise these goals to the local community. Send out invitations or sell tickets on an event website.

Pop-up Questions

1 What should you do first when planning a charity event?
2 What should you do if your company can afford it?

B **Listen to the talk and answer the questions.** 🔊 05-2

1 **Who will plan the event?**
   a. Deepak   b. Faridah   c. Trisha

2 **What will company employees receive?**
   a. registration forms   b. donations   c. medicine

3 **What will the company pay for?**
   a. admission   b. T-shirts   c. running shoes

Vocabulary

Ⓐ Learn some charity events.

	Word	Definition
1	live auction	a sales event led by an auctioneer in which participants bid on items
2	silent auction	a sales event in which participants write down their bids for items
3	online auction	a sales event in which participants place bids online rather than in person
4	gala	a large party that celebrates a success or a cause
5	art exhibit	an event in which art is displayed or sold
6	concert	a live music performance
7	sporting event	an event that features athletic competitions
8	fun run / walkathon	a noncompetitive run or walk that benefits a cause
9	festival / fair	a gathering that may feature games, competitions, music, food, and more

Ⓑ Complete the sentences with the words in the box.

sporting event	concert	fun run	art exhibit
fair	online auction	silent auction	live auction

1 We need to hire an auctioneer for the _____.

2 Several bands are going to perform at the _____ tomorrow.

3 Last year's _____ was a professional basketball game.

4 There will be food, rides, and a petting zoo at the _____.

5 We should collect some artwork for the _____ next month.

6 Register on this website if you want to participate in the _____.

7 The _____ will take place on the trails in West Park.

8 You don't need an auctioneer for a _____.

42

Speak Up

Practice the conversation with your partner by using the information in each memo. 🔊 05-3

Example

Event: gala for Save the Seals
When: late August
Where: San Fernando Hotel

To Do:
Book the venue - Marsha
Plan the menu - Stephan
Set up a website - Ricardo

Memo 1

Event: concert for Children of Tomorrow
When: early September
Where: Adaline Theater

To Do:
Book the venue – Kara
Reach out to musicians – Henry
Sell tickets – Winston

Memo 2

Event: fun run for St. Joseph's Hospital
When: late June
Where: Westmount Stadium

To Do:
Book the venue - Hong
Send registration forms - Milly
Advertise the event - Jin

Memo 3

Event: silent auction for Global Education
When: early February
Where: Prince Art Gallery

To Do:
Book the venue - Akemi
Reach out to donors - Paulo
Set up a website - Anita

A Hi, Marsha. The CEO asked us to plan a charity event.

B That's great. What type of event?

A It's a gala for Save the Seals.

B When will it take place?

A In late August at the San Fernando Hotel.

B Okay. I will book the venue.

A Great. Can you ask Stephan to plan the menu?

B Sure. We should also set up a website.

A Good idea. I think Ricardo has the most experience with that.

B I'll stop by his/her office to let him/her know.

! Tips for Success

When planning an event, delegate each task to the employee who has the most experience or knowledge of that task.

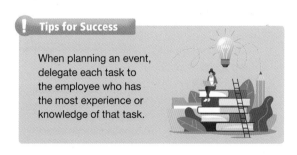

GRAMMAR

A **Let's learn about to-infinitives to show the purpose of an action.**

Positive	Interrogative
I stopped by his office **to tell** him the news.	Are you saving money **to buy** a car?
She went there **to meet** her new clients.	Did you go to the café **to meet** the client?
Mr. Jones went to the manager's office **to ask** for a raise.	Will he call us **to place** another order?
The manager took a long vacation **to relax**.	Can you call the client **to reschedule** the meeting?

B **Complete the following sentences by using the words in the box. Change the forms of the verbs to to-infinitives.**

eat	accept	let	get	ask	change	relax	look

1 Janette Hunter called me _____ me know the budget.

2 Did you write to Mr. Harrington _____ the job offer?

3 I think Sally went to the café _____ lunch.

4 Will you go to the job fair _____ for a new job?

5 The new hires stopped by my office _____ their ID cards.

6 They went to the meeting _____ for a raise.

7 Are you taking time off _____ this summer?

8 Did you call the client _____ the meeting time?

Know-how *at* **Work**   **How to Advertise a Charity Event**

Advertising is important for charity events. Without proper advertising, you may not reach your goals. There are a few important ways to advertise your event.

1   Set up an event website. Update it regularly with information about your event. In the case of an auction, showcase the items prior to the event.

2   Use social media to advertise. Make sure your event has a short, catchy name. Create a hashtag and encourage others to post about the event.

3   Advertise your event at trade shows, festivals, or markets. Hand out flyers with information about your event. Provide a signup sheet and collect email addresses.

4   Ask local businesses to sponsor your event. Add the sponsor's name and business logo to all your promotional materials. Encourage your sponsors to advertise your event on their websites and in stores.

5   Send invitations to your event. It's cheap and effective to send them by email. Make sure your invitations include the event information and the cost of admission if you plan to sell tickets.

Situation ②

A **Henrietta Cross gets an email from Benjamin Morris about a problem with the event. Read the email.**

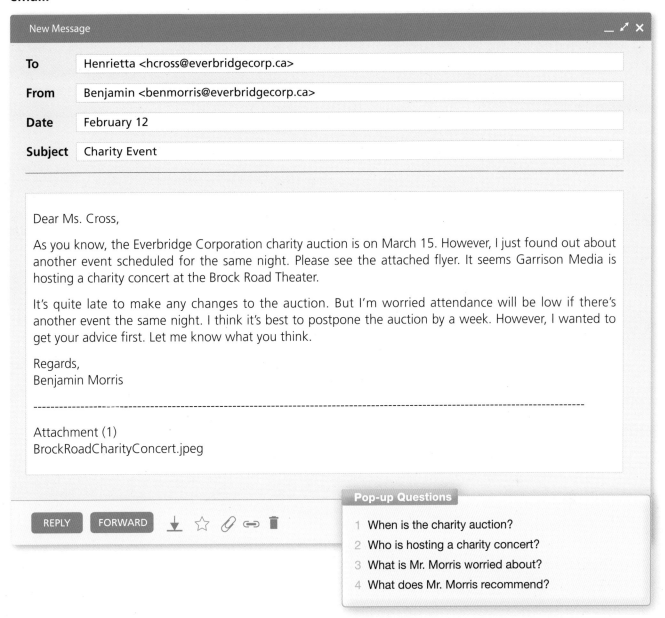

New Message   _ ↗ ✕

To	Henrietta <hcross@everbridgecorp.ca>
From	Benjamin <benmorris@everbridgecorp.ca>
Date	February 12
Subject	Charity Event

Dear Ms. Cross,

As you know, the Everbridge Corporation charity auction is on March 15. However, I just found out about another event scheduled for the same night. Please see the attached flyer. It seems Garrison Media is hosting a charity concert at the Brock Road Theater.

It's quite late to make any changes to the auction. But I'm worried attendance will be low if there's another event the same night. I think it's best to postpone the auction by a week. However, I wanted to get your advice first. Let me know what you think.

Regards,
Benjamin Morris

Attachment (1)
BrockRoadCharityConcert.jpeg

REPLY   FORWARD   ↓ ☆ 🖉 🔗 🗑

Pop-up Questions

1   When is the charity auction?

2   Who is hosting a charity concert?

3   What is Mr. Morris worried about?

4   What does Mr. Morris recommend?

B **Problem Solving :: Henrietta Cross gets a call from the venue manager letting her know the venue booking cannot be changed. Find a partner and choose the roles of Henrietta Cross and the venue manager. Then, role-play to discuss a possible solution. Use the information from the email in A if necessary.**

 **Useful Expressions**

A **Let's learn some expressions to use in business.**

When proposing a possible solution	When accepting or rejecting a proposed solution
I think it's best to postpone the auction.	I suppose that will work.
I recommend rescheduling the training session.	I think that's a good idea.
Let's gather some customer feedback first.	I'm not sure that will work.
I believe it's important to lower our prices.	I don't think we can do that.

When adding contradictory information	When asking for advice
But I'm worried attendance will be low.	I wanted to get your advice first.
However, the price is too high.	Could I get your opinion on something?
On the other hand, this office is very large.	I was wondering if you had any thoughts on the matter.

B **Fill in the blanks with the correct answers from the box. Then, practice the conversation with a partner.** 🔊 05-4

> I don't think we can do that
> Could I get your opinion on something
>
> However, I'm worried attendance will be low
> I think it's best to postpone the concert

A Hello, Terry. This is Bob Dawson calling.

B Hi, Mr. Dawson. How are you doing?

A I'm great. Thanks. ¹ _____?

B Sure. What's going on?

A Well, there's a charity gala the same night as our concert.

B I see. I wasn't aware of that.

A ² _____.

B Hmm. ³ _____.

A I know it's late to make changes to the schedule. ⁴ _____.

B That's true. Let me look into it, and I'll call you back.

A Okay. I'll talk to you soon.

Extra Practice

Role-play with your partner. One person proposes a solution to a problem. The other person accepts or rejects the solution.

A Hi. Could I get your opinion on something?

B Sure. What's going on?

A I think we need to reschedule the charity fun run.

B I suppose that will work.

Situation 3

Henrietta Cross gets an email from her boss regarding the charity event. Read the email and see if the results are positive or negative.

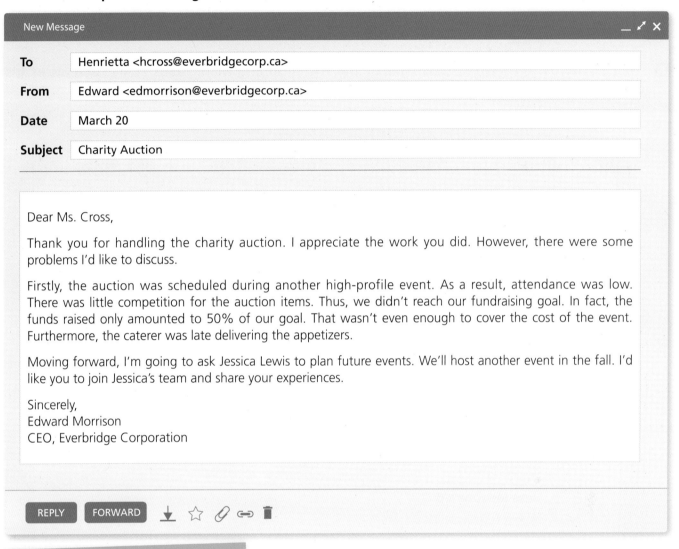

New Message

To	Henrietta <hcross@everbridgecorp.ca>
From	Edward <edmorrison@everbridgecorp.ca>
Date	March 20
Subject	Charity Auction

Dear Ms. Cross,

Thank you for handling the charity auction. I appreciate the work you did. However, there were some problems I'd like to discuss.

Firstly, the auction was scheduled during another high-profile event. As a result, attendance was low. There was little competition for the auction items. Thus, we didn't reach our fundraising goal. In fact, the funds raised only amounted to 50% of our goal. That wasn't even enough to cover the cost of the event. Furthermore, the caterer was late delivering the appetizers.

Moving forward, I'm going to ask Jessica Lewis to plan future events. We'll host another event in the fall. I'd like you to join Jessica's team and share your experiences.

Sincerely,
Edward Morrison
CEO, Everbridge Corporation

REPLY   FORWARD

Business English Dos and Don'ts

When providing negative feedback to an employee, there are a few things to consider. Clearly outline the problems. Don't use overly emotional phrases.

Dos
- The auction was scheduled during another event. (*clear*)
- The caterer was late delivering the appetizers. (*clear*)

Don'ts
- ✗ The scheduling conflict was infuriating. (*emotional*)
- ✗ The guests were practically starving to death! (*dramatic*)

Explain the effects of each problem simply and clearly.

Dos
- As a result, attendance was low. (*simple*)
- Thus, we didn't reach our fundraising goal. (*simple*)

Don'ts
- ✗ Because of this poor planning, many people chose to... (*too long*)
- ✗ We didn't raise nearly enough funds, so as a result, we... (*too long*)

Situation ①

A Colin Reynolds, the general manager of the HA Shopping Mall, reads some reviews of his company's app. Read the reviews.

Carla Fernando
★★☆☆☆ June 24

I used to love this app. But the latest update messed everything up. I used to be able to save items to my wish list easily. Now, I can only add ten items. Plus, the items get deleted after only a few days. That means I have to search for everything all over again. It's frustrating to say the least.

Ron Henderson
★☆☆☆☆ June 22

The app is unusable on mobile. It often freezes and closes without warning. I've made several reports. But nobody has ever replied to any of them. I don't recommend this app.

Jess MacDonald
★★☆☆☆ June 21

The update didn't seem to fix anything. There are still no international shipping options at checkout. It's unfortunate because I used to place an order once a month. The products are hard to find in my country! I hope it's fixed soon.

Tom Price
★☆☆☆☆ June 21

Absolutely terrible! Every update deletes all my payment information.

Pop-up Questions

1 What does Ms. Fernando write about the update?

2 How many items can Ms. Fernando add to her wish list?

3 What is Mr. Henderson's problem with the app?

4 What does Ms. MacDonald hope for?

B Take Notes :: Based on the reviews in A, complete the memo.

Negative Customer Experiences - June

Wish List:
- can only add ten items
- items get ¹_____ after only
  a few days

Mobile:
- freezes and closes without warning
- nobody ²_____ reports

Checkout:
- no ³_____ shipping options

Customer Info:
- every update deletes ⁴_____

Background Knowledge

A Read and learn about dealing with customer complaints.

Customer feedback is important for many businesses. Negative feedback is especially important. It helps companies identify problems. It also gives employees an opportunity to solve issues and to improve their overall business practices. There are a few ways to collect negative feedback.

Many companies accept complaints over the phone. Customer service staff members should be trained to handle these complaints. They must listen carefully, ask thoughtful questions, and use an apologetic tone. Customer service staff members should also be knowledgeable. They may not be able to solve a problem immediately. But they should try their best to satisfy their customers' needs.

Nowadays, many companies receive online complaints. Additionally, negative reviews can provide a wide variety of feedback about products and services. By using reviews, companies can pinpoint trends in customer experiences. They can then come up with strategies on how to best serve their customers.

Pop-up Questions

1 Why is negative feedback especially important?
2 What can negative reviews provide?

B Listen to the talk and answer the questions. 06-1

1 **What did several customers have trouble with?**
   a. the wish list
   b. international shipping
   c. the advertisements

2 **What does the app do since the last update?**
   a. saves items
   b. freezes and closes
   c. sends reports

3 **Who works in the IT Department?**
   a. Leon
   b. Natalie
   c. Denise

Vocabulary

A Let's learn some words related to customer complaints.

review

application

troubleshoot

make a complaint

IT Department

brand

rate

update

B Choose the correct answer for each blank.

1 If you like the product, please leave a positive _____.
   a. brand   b. review   c. update   d. troubleshoot

2 Caroline worked in the _____ for about five years.
   a. review   b. rate   c. IT Department   d. application

3 This logo represents the company's unique _____.
   a. update   b. review   c. troubleshoot   d. brand

4 They are in the process of developing a new mobile _____.
   a. application   b. IT Department   c. rate   d. review

5 Jeffrey was so upset. He called the company to _____.
   a. update   b. troubleshoot
   c. brand   d. make a complaint

6 The next _____ should fix most of the problems.
   a. rate   b. update
   c. make a complaint   d. brand

Speak Up

Practice the conversation with your partner by using the information in each memo. 🔊 06-2

Example

SJ Fashion Sense

Negative Customer Experiences
- August

Wish List - most items are not saved

Check-out - the discount codes are not working

Mobile App - it won't open after the last update

Memo 1

AZ Games

Negative Customer Experiences
- February

Customer Info - the last update deleted order histories

Advertisements - there are too many of them

Mobile App - nobody replied to reports

Memo 2

Home Expressions

Negative Customer Experiences
- June

Wish List - customers can only add twenty items

Check-out - there are no international shipping options

Mobile App - it closes without warning

Memo 3

Clover Pharmaceuticals

Negative Customer Experiences
- October

Customer Info - every update deletes payment information

Advertisements - they cause the app to freeze

Mobile App - the notifications aren't working

A Hi, Adiba. I've been reading some customer reviews for the month of August.
This is a list of common problems.

B It looks like there's an issue with the wish list.

A Right. It seems most items are not saved.

B What else is happening?

A Well, there's a problem with the checkout.
The discount codes are not working.

B I'm sure the IT Department can fix that.

A There's also an issue with the mobile app.

B I see that. I guess it won't open after the last update.

> **! Tips for Success**
>
> When analyzing customer feedback, make a list of commonly reported problems. Then, discuss possible solutions.

GRAMMAR

A **Let's learn about the present perfect continuous tense.**

have/has been + verb -ing	have/has not been + verb -ing
I**'ve been reading** some customer reviews.	He **hasn't been submitting** his reports on time.
He **has been working** late all week.	The company's CEO **hasn't been feeling** well.
The team **has been contacting** clients all morning.	Madeline **hasn't been studying** for her exam.
You**'ve been traveling** a lot lately.	You **haven't been working** here for very long.

B **Complete the following sentences by using the verbs in parenthesis. Change the verbs to the present perfect continuous tense.**

1 Henry _____ at the company for 10 years. (work)

2 The customer _____ the problem for an hour. (discuss)

3 Amanda and Joe _____ in France all summer. (travel)

4 The receptionist _____ the phones correctly. (not + answer)

5 I _____ about this problem all morning. (think)

6 The Customer Service Department _____ reviews. (not + read)

7 The cleaning staff _____ the cafeteria floor. (not + wash)

8 The manager _____ our progress carefully. (watch)

📶 Know-how *at* **Work**   **How to Manage Your Online Brand**

Many customers read reviews before purchasing a product or a service. Thus, reviews and ratings can make or break your business. It's important to manage your online brand.

1 Read as many online reviews as possible. Take note of positive reviews to identify what's working for your company. Gather negative feedback as well. Use it to implement changes or to improve your policies.

2 Take complaints seriously and respond to as many as possible. Ensure your responses are thoughtful and professional. Instead of getting defensive, offer your customers realistic solutions.

3 Research widely. Your company might appear on many different websites and social networking services. Visit a wide variety of platforms to gather feedback.

4 If your company can afford it, hire a community manager. Community managers specialize in monitoring your online brand. They can help your company respond to problems as well as analyze customer feedback.

Situation ②

A Colin Reynolds meets with Tina O'Reilly, Nelson Long, and Stefano Russo from the IT Department to discuss some problems with the company's app. Read the conversation. 06-3

C   Hello, everyone. I assume you all saw my memo. Some of the customers mentioned they can only add ten items to their wish lists. They also said the items get deleted after a few days.

T   I can handle that. It will just be a minor adjustment.

C   Good to hear. A few customers mentioned problems during payment. Apparently, there are no international shipping options.

N   I'll fix that.

C   Okay. Normally, the app saves preferred payment options, too. But every time we launch an update, that information disappears. Can we do anything about that?

N   Yes. I'll make sure that doesn't happen again.

C   Great. One last thing. When we launch the next update, we're going to post an announcement. Stefano, can you draft that?

S   No problem. We should also inform some of the customers directly. Someone in the Customer Service Department should reply to some of the reviews.

C   That's an excellent idea.

Pop-up Questions

1 What problem will Ms. O'Reilly handle?
2 What does Mr. Reynolds say about shipping?
3 What happens during each update?
4 What will Mr. Russo do?

B **Problem Solving ::** Colin Reynolds calls Chang He in Customer Service to ask her to reply to some customer reviews. Find a partner and choose the roles of Colin Reynolds and Chang He. Then, role-play to discuss a possible solution. Use the information from the conversation in A if necessary.

A **Let's learn some expressions to use in business.**

When starting a meeting	When giving employees assignments
Hello, everyone. I assume you all saw my memo.	Stefano, can you draft that?
Thank you for joining me on such short notice.	Can you handle that, Richard?
Take a seat, everyone. Let's begin.	I'd like you to work on that, Beth.
Good afternoon. Make yourselves comfortable.	Mitchell, please take care of that.
When replying to orders	**When volunteering to solve a problem**
Yes. I'll make sure it doesn't happen again.	I can handle that.
No problem. I'll start right away.	I'll fix that.
Of course. It won't take very long.	Let me deal with it.

B **Fill in the blanks with the correct answers from the box. Then, practice the conversation with a partner.** 🔊 06-4

I'd like you to work on that	I'll start right away
I'll fix that	Thank you for joining me

A Hi, Spencer. ¹_____ on such short notice.

B Of course. What's been going on?

A I've been analyzing customer feedback. There are a few problems with our mobile app.

B I see. Like what?

A Apparently, the advertisements cause the app to freeze.

B ²_____. It won't take very long.

A In addition, the notifications aren't working. ³_____.

B No problem. ⁴_____.

A Thanks, Spencer. Let me know if you need any help.

B Will do.

Extra Practice

Role-play with your partner. A manager gives an employee an assignment. The employee accepts the assignment.

A There's a problem with our mobile app.

B I saw that. The discount codes aren't working.

A Can you take care of that?

B Of course. It won't take very long.

Situation 3

Colin Reynolds sees an announcement regarding his company's latest app update. Read the webpage and see if the results are positive or negative.

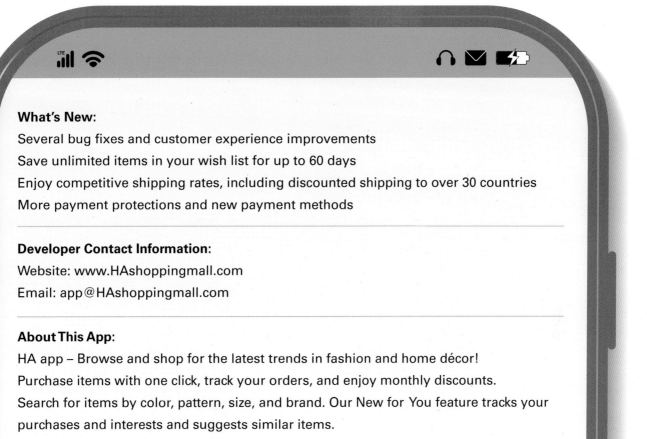

What's New:

Several bug fixes and customer experience improvements

Save unlimited items in your wish list for up to 60 days

Enjoy competitive shipping rates, including discounted shipping to over 30 countries

More payment protections and new payment methods

Developer Contact Information:

Website: www.HAshoppingmall.com

Email: app@HAshoppingmall.com

About This App:

HA app – Browse and shop for the latest trends in fashion and home décor!

Purchase items with one click, track your orders, and enjoy monthly discounts.

Search for items by color, pattern, size, and brand. Our New for You feature tracks your purchases and interests and suggests similar items.

Business English Dos and Don'ts

When providing an online summary about your company, there are a few things to consider. Summarize what your customers can do with specific details.

Dos

- ○ Browse and shop for the latest trends in fashion and home décor! (*detailed*)
- ○ Purchase items with one click, track your orders, and enjoy monthly discounts. (*detailed*)

Don'ts

- ✗ Search for all the items you need. (*not specific*)
- ✗ Buy and sell items and receive discounts once in a while. (*not specific*)

Introduce and explain new features. Mention what each new feature does.

Dos

- ○ Our New for You feature tracks your purchases and interests and suggests similar items. (*detailed*)
- ○ Download the Better Sales app and purchase discounted items on your phone or computer. (*detailed*)

Don'ts

- ✗ Our new features will improve your shopping experience. (*unclear*)
- ✗ Get the app and use it wherever you are. (*unclear*)

Situation ❶

A **Wesley Wallace gets an email from the chief sales officer asking him to lead a meeting. Read the email.**

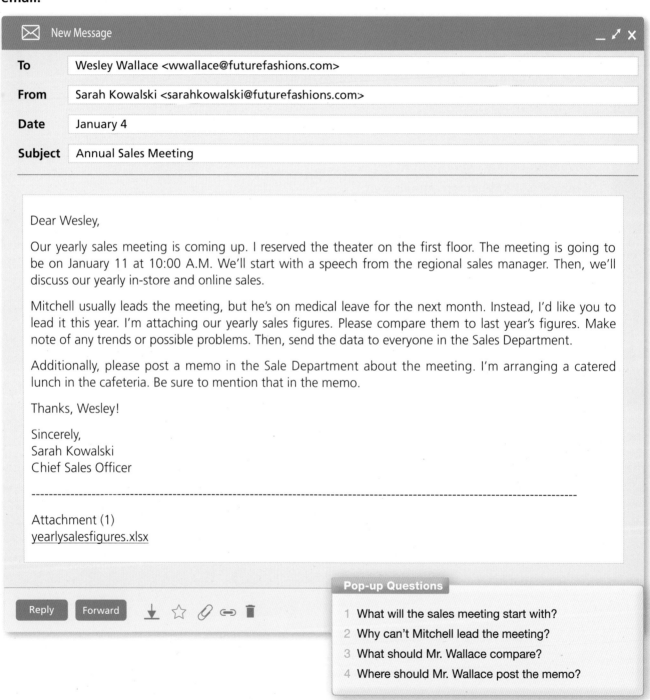

✉ New Message   _ ↗ ✕

To	Wesley Wallace <wwallace@futurefashions.com>
From	Sarah Kowalski <sarahkowalski@futurefashions.com>
Date	January 4
Subject	Annual Sales Meeting

Dear Wesley,

Our yearly sales meeting is coming up. I reserved the theater on the first floor. The meeting is going to be on January 11 at 10:00 A.M. We'll start with a speech from the regional sales manager. Then, we'll discuss our yearly in-store and online sales.

Mitchell usually leads the meeting, but he's on medical leave for the next month. Instead, I'd like you to lead it this year. I'm attaching our yearly sales figures. Please compare them to last year's figures. Make note of any trends or possible problems. Then, send the data to everyone in the Sales Department.

Additionally, please post a memo in the Sale Department about the meeting. I'm arranging a catered lunch in the cafeteria. Be sure to mention that in the memo.

Thanks, Wesley!

Sincerely,
Sarah Kowalski
Chief Sales Officer

Attachment (1)
yearlysalesfigures.xlsx

[Reply] [Forward]   ↓ ☆ 🖉 🔗 🗑

Pop-up Questions

1 What will the sales meeting start with?

2 Why can't Mitchell lead the meeting?

3 What should Mr. Wallace compare?

4 Where should Mr. Wallace post the memo?

B **Take Notes :: Based on the email in A, complete the memo.**

Date: January 7

To: ¹ _____ employees   From: Wesley Wallace, Assistant Manager

Subject: Annual ² _____

We will have our annual sales meeting on Friday, ³ _____ . Please come to the ⁴ _____ on the first floor at ⁵ _____ . The regional manager, Henry Camp, will give ⁶ _____ . Then, we will discuss our ⁷ _____ . A ⁸ _____ in the cafeteria will follow.

Please review the information packet prior to the meeting. If you did not receive one, stop by my office.

Background Knowledge

A **Read and learn about sales meetings.**

Sales meetings are essential for many companies. During a sales meeting, employees gather to discuss various issues pertaining to the Sales Department. Usually, a manager or a company executive leads the meeting. Employees from other departments might also join.

Sales meetings may occur weekly, monthly, or even yearly. There are several reasons to schedule a sales meeting. During the meeting, representatives often discuss challenges. They also brainstorm solutions. Sales meetings are a great time to introduce new products and services. Managers should make sure to celebrate successes, too.

It can be expensive to hold regular sales meetings. Having too many can also decrease employee productivity. Managers should schedule sales meetings only when necessary. That way, sales representatives can spend more time focusing on their work.

Pop-up Questions

1 Who usually leads a sales meeting?
2 What can having too many sales meetings do?

B **Listen to the talk and answer the questions.** 🔊 07-1

1 **Who will lead the monthly sales meeting?**
   a. Olga   b. Jeremiah   c. Dennis

2 **What should the sales figures be compared to?**
   a. last year's sales   b. last month's sales   c. January's sales

3 **Where does the man say to post the memo?**
   a. in conference room 306   b. in the cafeteria   c. in the Sales Department

Vocabulary

A Let's learn some words related to sales meetings.

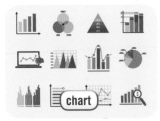  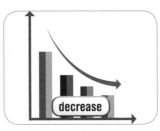 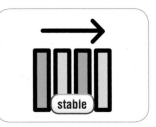

B Choose the correct answer for each blank.

1 There wasn't a big change. Our online sales have been _____ for six months.
   a. compare　　　　b. chart　　　　c. stable　　　　d. presentation

2 Since Victoria is away, I would like you to give a(n) _____ at the meeting.
   a. presentation　　b. increase　　　c. chart　　　　d. decrease

3 Please take a look at this _____. As you can see, exports have increased.
   a. decrease　　　　b. stable　　　　c. online sales　　d. chart

4 I think we should hire a social media _____ before we launch the product.
   a. presentation　　b. compare　　　c. chart　　　　d. consultant

5 Did you look at the sales figures? How were last month's _____?
   a. increase　　　　b. online sales　　c. presentation　　d. compare

6 He thinks our profits will _____ a lot this year. This could be a big problem.
   a. decrease　　　　b. social media　　c. increase　　　d. stable

Speak Up

Practice the conversation with your partner by using the information in each memo. 🔊 07-2

(Example)

Date January 20   **To** Finance Department employees   **From** Chloe Mason
Subject Annual Budget Meeting

We will have our annual budget meeting on Wednesday, January 20. Please come to conference room 205 on the second floor at 9:00 A.M. The CFO, Nelson Adams, will give a speech. Then, we will discuss our yearly budget. Lunch at Rico's Grill House will follow.

(Memo 1)

Date January 5   **To** Marketing Department employees   **From** Joon Han
Subject Annual Marketing Meeting

We will have our annual marketing meeting on Monday, January 5. Please come to the auditorium on the first floor at 9:30 A.M. The CMO, Jean Philips, will give a speech. Then, we will discuss our yearly marketing plan. Lunch at La Cove Restaurant will follow.

(Memo 2)

Date January 8   **To** Sales Department employees   **From** Louis Bastien
Subject Annual Sales Meeting

We will have our annual sales meeting on Thursday, January 8. Please come to conference room 301 on the third floor at 10:00 A.M. The CSO, Simone Woods, will give a speech. Then, we will discuss our yearly sales plan. Lunch at Thai Sky Restaurant will follow.

A Hi there, Chloe. Our yearly budget meeting is coming up.

B It's this month, right?

A Yes, on January 20 at 9:00 A.M.

B Oh, that's soon.

A I'd like you to draft a memo about it.

   I've already reserved conference room 205.

B Okay. I'll post a memo in the Finance Department.

A Mention that Nelson Adams will give a speech.

B Sure. Is there anything else?

A Yes. I want to host a lunch at Rico's Grill House after.

B I'll make the reservation as well.

! Tips for Success

When drafting a memo about an upcoming meeting, list the date, the time, the location, and any other important details of the event.

 **GRAMMAR**

A **Let's learn about collocations.**

give	make	take
He will **give a speech** tomorrow. She **gave a description** of the missing bag. Mr. Brown **gave notice** that he will quit. The CEO will **give more information** at the meeting.	Can you **make a reservation**? Let's **make an appointment** with the client. They **made a deal** last fall. Vanessa **made a mistake** and had to apologize.	Sandra will **take a taxi** to the airport instead. Can you **take a look** at this chart? If you're sick, **take some medicine**. We **took a vacation** last summer.

B **Complete the following sentences by using** *give*, *make*, **or** *take*. **Change the verbs to their past tense forms if necessary.**

1 The CEO _____ a decision last week.

2 Bethany _____ notes during his speech.

3 He _____ me a great idea at the meeting.

4 We should _____ an effort to train him.

5 Hello, everyone. Please _____ a seat.

6 Did you _____ the client an offer yet?

7 Will Rita _____ part in the training session?

8 Mr. Thompson will _____ me advice about my career.

∿ Know-how *at* **Work**   **How to Prepare for a Sales Meeting**

Preparation is very important when it comes to sales meetings. Prior to leading a sales meeting, there are several things you must do to ensure your meeting is successful.

1 Gather information before the meeting. This may include monthly or yearly sales figures. It may also include predictions for future sales. Create attractive graphs or charts to display the data.

2 Give the attendees roles during the meeting. Ask someone to record the minutes for each meeting. Prior to the meeting, ask sales representatives to share their pitches. Encourage others to share any ideas they have and any obstacles they've encountered.

3 Send materials in advance. This includes any charts, graphs, or sales figures. It also includes a summary of what will be discussed during the meeting. This will give the attendees a chance to prepare as well.

4 Ensure everything is set up prior to the meeting. Visit the room you will use. Make sure that the equipment works and that there are enough chairs for everyone. Check that you have all the files and information you will use.

Situation ②

A Wesley Wallace is presenting the yearly sales figures at the annual meeting. Read the presentation and chart. ◀» 07-3

That concludes our in-store sales figures. Let's move on to online sales. There were no significant changes in footwear. However, take a look at our online clothing sales. This chart compares this year's sales with last year's.

As you can see, baby and children's clothing sales increased. There was a slight decrease in men's clothing sales. The most alarming change was in women's clothing. Sales dropped significantly this year. However, our in-store sales remained the same. So this isn't a case of customers preferring to shop in person. We're simply losing their business.

I spoke with the Customer Service Department. Shelly Bent was kind enough to compile a list of common customer complaints. Let's look at the complaints now and brainstorm possible solutions.

Online Fashion Sales

Legend: Last Year | This Year

Pop-up Questions

1 What is Mr. Wallace discussing?
2 What increased over the last year?
3 What remained the same?
4 What did Ms. Bent do?

B Problem Solving :: Wesley Wallace calls Shelly Bent to ask for more information about the customer complaints. Find a partner and choose the roles of Wesley Wallace and Shelly Bent. Then, role-play to discuss a possible solution. Use the information from the presentation in A if necessary.

A **Let's learn some expressions to use in business.**

When changing topics during a presentation	When explaining a drastic change
Let's move on to online sales.	The most alarming change was in women's clothing.
Next on the agenda is the advertising budget.	Sales dropped significantly this year.
Now I'd like to share last month's sales figures.	We've seen a disturbing decrease in online sales.
Let's change direction and talk about the complaints.	We lost a substantial number of clients.
When drawing attention to data	**When making conclusions**
Take a look at our online clothing sales.	We're simply losing their business.
This chart shows our profits from last year.	Our clients are obviously unhappy.
Turn to the chart on page 3 for specific numbers.	We definitely need to solve this issue.

B **Fill in the blanks with the correct answers from the box. Then, practice the conversation with a partner.** 🔊 07-4

This chart shows our profits from	Our customers are obviously unhappy
Exports dropped significantly in the summer	Let's move on to international sales

A That concludes our look at our national sales.

B Thanks, Jared. ¹_____.

A Sure, Lynn. ²_____ the beginning of last year.

B As you can see, there were no significant decreases. Exports were stable from January to April.

A Now take a look at the rest of the year.

B ³_____. There was a slight increase in fall, and then there was another drop in winter.

A Jared and I both agree. ⁴_____.

B The problem might be the cost of shipping.

A That's right. The cost increased a lot last year.

Extra Practice

Role-play with your partner. Two employees are doing a presentation. One employee mentions a drop in sales. The other employee makes a conclusion.

A Take a look at our online sales.

B We've seen a disturbing decrease.

A However, our in-store sales remained stable.

B That's right. We're simply losing our online customers.

Situation 3

Wesley Wallace gets an email from the chief marketing officer. Read the email and see if the results are positive or negative.

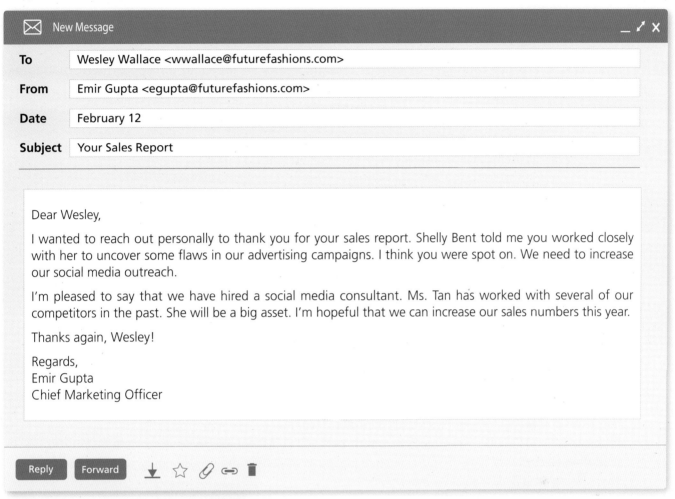

To	Wesley Wallace <wwallace@futurefashions.com>
From	Emir Gupta <egupta@futurefashions.com>
Date	February 12
Subject	Your Sales Report

Dear Wesley,

I wanted to reach out personally to thank you for your sales report. Shelly Bent told me you worked closely with her to uncover some flaws in our advertising campaigns. I think you were spot on. We need to increase our social media outreach.

I'm pleased to say that we have hired a social media consultant. Ms. Tan has worked with several of our competitors in the past. She will be a big asset. I'm hopeful that we can increase our sales numbers this year.

Thanks again, Wesley!

Regards,
Emir Gupta
Chief Marketing Officer

Business English Dos and Don'ts

When explaining a change in business tactics, there are a few important things to remember. Clearly explain what the change is and why it must occur.

Dos

○ We need to increase our social media outreach. (*clear*)
○ I'm pleased to say that we have hired a social media consultant. (*clear*)

Don'ts

✕ We're going to make some important changes in the future. (*unclear*)
✕ We'll hire someone to deal with the issue. (*unclear*)

Make positive predictions regarding the change. Try to avoid negative statements.

Dos

○ She will be a big asset. (*positive*)
○ I'm hopeful that we can increase our sales numbers this year. (*positive*)

Don'ts

✕ I'm not sure if she'll fit in here. (*negative*)
✕ We'd better increase our sales, or we'll get fired. (*negative*)

Moving to a New Office

Situation ❶

Ⓐ William Park, the office manager of Broker Design, sends an email to all department managers. Read the email.

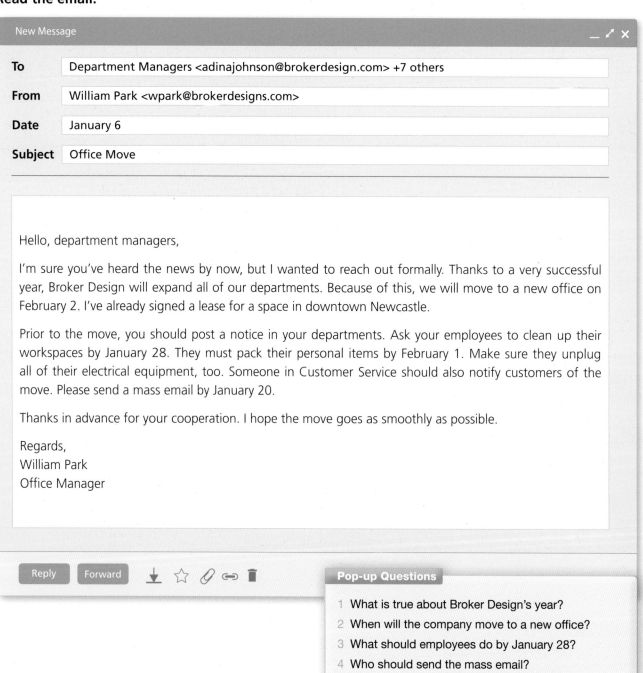

New Message ─ ⤢ ✕

To	Department Managers <adinajohnson@brokerdesign.com> +7 others
From	William Park <wpark@brokerdesigns.com>
Date	January 6
Subject	Office Move

Hello, department managers,

I'm sure you've heard the news by now, but I wanted to reach out formally. Thanks to a very successful year, Broker Design will expand all of our departments. Because of this, we will move to a new office on February 2. I've already signed a lease for a space in downtown Newcastle.

Prior to the move, you should post a notice in your departments. Ask your employees to clean up their workspaces by January 28. They must pack their personal items by February 1. Make sure they unplug all of their electrical equipment, too. Someone in Customer Service should also notify customers of the move. Please send a mass email by January 20.

Thanks in advance for your cooperation. I hope the move goes as smoothly as possible.

Regards,
William Park
Office Manager

Reply   Forward   ↓ ☆ ⧉ ⊷ 🗑

Pop-up Questions

1 What is true about Broker Design's year?

2 When will the company move to a new office?

3 What should employees do by January 28?

4 Who should send the mass email?

B Take Notes :: Based on the email in A, complete the notice.

Announcement – Office Move

We're moving to a new office in downtown [1] _____ on [2] _____ !

Prior to the move, make sure you:

- Clean up your workspace by [3] _____
- Pack your [4] _____ by February 1
- Unplug all of your [5] _____ as well
- [6] _____ – Tyrone Prince will send a mass email on [7] _____

Thank you for cooperation!

Background Knowledge

A Read and learn about reasons for moving to a new office.

There are many reasons to move to a new office space. Expansion is the most common reason. Some companies experience rapid growth. They hire many new employees. A larger office is needed to accommodate them. Sometimes companies have 2 or 3 separate offices. Merging them into one large office is common.

Cost is also an important reason for moving. Some locations are more expensive than others. If a company does not generate enough business, it might not be able to renew an expensive lease. In that case, it's common to move to a less expensive location.

Additionally, companies must consider their customers. Many businesses move to a new location to be closer to their customers. They might also move to an area where they can attract new customers. Changing locations benefits employees, too. It gives them a fresh start and can boost productivity.

Pop-up Questions

1 What is the most common reason to move to a new office space?

2 Why might a company move to a less expensive location?

B Listen to the talk and answer the questions. (◄» 08-1)

1 **What is the main reason for the move?**

a. low sales numbers   b. too many employees   c. damaged floors

2 **What does the woman ask the managers to do?**

a. sign a lease   b. post notices   c. let employees go

3 **When should employees clean up their workspaces by?**

a. March 5   b. March 9   c. March 10

Vocabulary

A **Learn some words related to moving.**

workspace

pack / unpack

unplug

furniture

lease

set up

decorate

update a website

B **Match each word with the correct definition.**

1 furniture •   • a. to change the décor of an office

2 workspace •   • b. to place items into a box before moving

3 decorate •   • c. to add new information to a webpage

4 unplug •   • d. items in an office, such as desks and chairs

5 pack •   • e. to remove plugs from electrical outlets

6 update a website •   • f. a person's work area, desk, or cubicle

7 lease •   • g. to put furniture, computers, etc. in position

8 set up •   • h. a contract signed in order to rent a space

Speak Up

Practice the conversation with your partner by using the information in each notice. 08-2

Example

We're moving to a new office in downtown Los Angeles on March 7!

Make sure you:

- Clean up workspaces by March 4
- Set up new workspaces by March 8
- Update the website before March 9

Notice 1

We're moving to a new office in downtown Vancouver on September 18!

Make sure you:

- Pack personal items by September 17
- Decorate the new office by September 20
- Send a mass email by September 18

Notice 2

We're moving to a new office in downtown London on April 11!

Make sure you:

- Clean up workspaces by April 9
- Pack personal items by April 10
- Call all our clients before April 11

Notice 3

We're moving to a new office in downtown Melbourne on February 5!

Make sure you:

- Pack personal items by February 4
- Unplug electrical equipment by February 4
- Send a mass text message by February 6

A Hi, Kelly. Have you heard the news?

B Yes, we're moving to a new office in downtown Los Angeles!

A That's right. The move is on March 7.

B There's a lot to do before the move.

A Can you contact the department managers?

B Sure. I'll ask them to post a notice.

A Employees must clean up their workspaces by March 4.

B Okay. Then they have to set up their new workspaces by March 8?

A Yes. We must also notify our clients of the move.

B Let's update the website before March 9.

> **! Tips for Success**
>
> When asking employees to do something via a notice, make sure to add deadlines for each task.

A **Let's learn about *must* and *have to*.**

must + infinitive	has/have to + infinitive
You **must submit** the forms by Friday at 5:00 P.M. We **must register** online for the seminar.	They **have to wear** uniforms at work. We **have to fly** to Chicago for the conference.
must + not + infinitive	**does/do + not + have to + infinitive**
You **must not eat** in the conference room. They **must not forget** their ID cards.	I **don't have to work** late tonight. Sally **doesn't have to meet** the client tomorrow.

*does/do not have to = does/do not need to

B **Fill in the blanks with the words in the box and in parentheses. Change the form of *have to* if necessary.**

apologize	finish	work	leave	turn	redo	speak	go

1 You _____ the project by May 3. (must)

2 I just talked to the manager. We _____ late tonight. (not + have to)

3 Everyone _____ to the training session next week. (have to)

4 Food and beverages _____ the breakroom. (must + not)

5 I can't hear you. You _____ a little louder. (must)

6 Luckily, she _____ the whole report. (not + have to)

7 Jim _____ to the client immediately for being rude. (must)

8 Mr. Nestor said it's cold. We _____ up the heat. (have to)

Know-how *at* Work   **How to Choose an Office Space**

Choosing the right office space is important for running a successful business. There are many options available, but there are a few ways to ensure an office space is right for your company.

1 Consider the cost of the space. Your company should be able to pay the rent without any trouble. Offices located downtown are usually quite expensive. Additionally, larger offices are expensive to heat and cool.

2 Choose an office space that your customers can easily reach. Additionally, it should be close to employees' homes. Otherwise, some employees might have to quit when the move happens.

3 Make sure to choose an office that can accommodate growth. If you plan to hire more employees, ensure there is enough space for them.

4 Take a tour of each office space before signing a lease. If the office space is in poor condition, it might need renovations. Renovating the space could be very expensive. It could also delay your moving date.

5 Choose an office with a layout that works for your company. Open spaces are great for modern companies. However, some companies are more traditional and prefer closed offices.

Situation ②

A William Park gets a call from Carlo Benson explaining a problem with the new office. Read the telephone conversation. 🔊 08-3

> 📞 **Carlo Benson** Hello, Mr. Park. This is Carlo from Ashmore Renovations. I have some unfortunate news to share.
>
> 📞 **William Park** What seems to be the problem?
>
> 📞 **Carlo Benson** We're in the middle of installing the new flooring in your office downtown.
>
> 📞 **William Park** Yes, what happened?
>
> 📞 **Carlo Benson** Well, we found a lot of water damage. I think there's a leaky pipe under the floor.
>
> 📞 **William Park** That's bad news indeed.
>
> 📞 **Carlo Benson** The wood is totally rotted. We have to replace it. We should also replace some of the pipes and check the walls for mold.
>
> 📞 **William Park** How long do you think it will take?
>
> 📞 **Carlo Benson** With damage like this, it's going to take at least three weeks.
>
> 📞 **William Park** So that puts our earliest moving date at February 23 or 24.
>
> 📞 **Carlo Benson** I think so. I've spoken to the building owner. Luckily, he has agreed to cover the cost of the repairs.
>
> 📞 **William Park** I guess it isn't all bad news then.
>
> 📞 **Carlo Benson** I'll keep you updated on our progress.
>
> 📞 **William Park** Thank you, Carlo.

Pop-up Questions

1. What company does Mr. Benson work for?
2. What is the problem with the floor?
3. How long will the repairs take?
4. Who will cover the cost of the repairs?

B **Problem Solving ::** William Park must call the owner of his current office building to ask if he can use the space for an additional three weeks. Find a partner and choose the roles of William Park and the building owner. Then, role-play to discuss a possible solution. Use the information from the telephone conversation in A if necessary.

A **Let's learn some expressions to use in business.**

When asking for an estimate	When making an estimate
How long do you think it will take?	That puts our earliest moving date at February 23 or 24.
Can you give me an estimate of the cost?	I assume it will cost around $300 to fix.
Do you think it will take longer than three weeks?	It's going to take at least three weeks.
Do you have any idea when it will happen?	I'm guessing the merger will happen in May.
When delivering bad news	**When responding to bad news**
I have some unfortunate news to share.	That's bad news indeed.
Unfortunately, we've had some setbacks.	That's disappointing.
Things are not going as planned.	How frustrating.

B **Fill in the blanks with the correct answers from the box. Then, practice the conversation with a partner.** ◀)) 08-4

do you think it will take longer	that's disappointing
that puts our earliest moving date at	I have some unfortunate news to share

A Hello, Ms. Jessop. This is Mark calling.

B Hi, Mark. How are you doing?

A Fine, thanks. But ¹ _____ .

B What happened?

A There are some problems with the wiring at your new office.

B I see. ² _____ .

A We have to replace the old wiring.

B ³ _____ than three weeks?

A Yes. It's going to take at least a month.

B Hmm. ⁴ _____ June 12 or 13.

A I think so.

B How frustrating. Thanks for letting me know, Mark.

Extra Practice

Role-play with your partner. One person mentions a problem with an office. The other person responds to the bad news.

A Hi, Ms. Jones. There is some water damage at your new office.

B Do you think it will take longer than two weeks to fix?

A It's going to take at least three weeks.

B That's bad news indeed.

Situation 3

William Park sees an update posted to the Broker Design website. Read the webpage and see if the results are positive or negative.

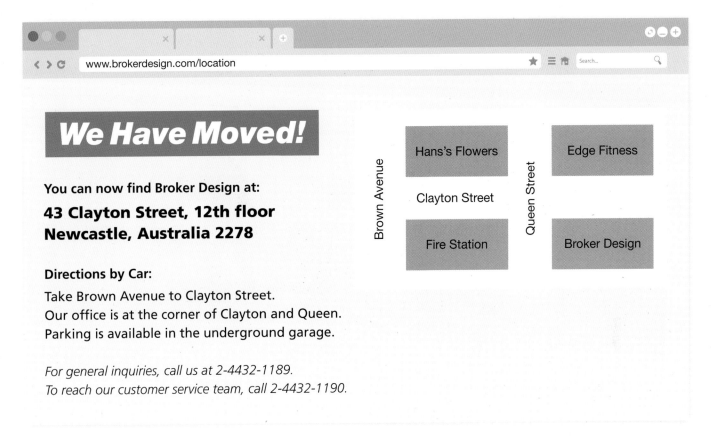

www.brokerdesign.com/location

We Have Moved!

You can now find Broker Design at:

**43 Clayton Street, 12th floor
Newcastle, Australia 2278**

Directions by Car:

Take Brown Avenue to Clayton Street.
Our office is at the corner of Clayton and Queen.
Parking is available in the underground garage.

For general inquiries, call us at 2-4432-1189.
To reach our customer service team, call 2-4432-1190.

Brown Avenue | Hans's Flowers | Queen Street | Edge Fitness
Clayton Street
Fire Station | Broker Design

Business English Dos and Don'ts

When updating a website after a move, make sure the information is clear and concise. Use short directions that are easy to read. Avoid long explanations.

Dos
- Take Brown Avenue to Clayton Street. (*short*)
- Parking is available in the underground garage. (*short*)

Don'ts
- ✕ Drive along Brown Avenue and then turn onto Clayton Street and travel west until you reach our office at the corner. (*too long*)
- ✕ There is parking available in the underground garage, but it may fill up, so taking public transit is a better choice. (*too long*)

Provide other ways to reach your company. Add relevant phone numbers or emails.

Dos
- For general inquiries, call us at 2-4432-1189. (*specific*)
- To reach our customer service team, call 2-4432-1190. (*specific*)

Don'ts
- ✕ If you have any questions or concerns, simply give us a call. (*not detailed enough*)
- ✕ We can be reached by telephone, by email, and on our website. (*not detailed enough*)

Situation ❶

A Cole Newberry and Yara Aman are discussing an announcement on the bulletin board. Read the conversation. 🔊 09-1

C Hi, Ms. Aman. Is this the promotion announcement?

Y It sure is.

C Oh, wow. You got promoted. Congratulations on becoming our next marketing manager!

Y Thank you! I'm very excited to start in January.

C I see Freddy O'Brien is now the assistant production manager.

Y You look disappointed.

C I was hoping to get the promotion myself.

Y I'm sorry to hear that.

C Thank you. I'll have to congratulate Freddy. He deserves it.

Y Has anyone spoken to Louise Fern?

C I'm not sure. Why?

Y She was promoted as well. She'll be the new shipping manager after Mr. Lewis retires at the end of April.

C The announcement was sent by email as well, wasn't it?

Y I'm not sure. Let me check.

Pop-up Questions

1 Who is the company's new marketing manager?
2 Why is Mr. Newberry disappointed?
3 When will Mr. Lewis retire?
4 What will Ms. Aman likely do next?

B **Take Notes ::** Based on the conversation in A, complete the promotion announcement.

Announcement: Promotions

Yara Aman	Louise Fern	Freddy O'Brien
promoted to [1] _____ manager effective January 1	promoted to [2] _____ manager effective [3] _____ 1	promoted to [4] _____ manager effective January 1

Background Knowledge

A **Read and learn about getting a promotion.**

Getting a promotion can be great for your career. Promotions often mean more responsibilities, but they also mean higher salaries and more benefits. Many employees want to get promoted, so it is important to stand out. There are a few ways you can do this.

Focus on forming good work relationships. It's important to be friendly with both your bosses and coworkers. Get to know them and try to share some of their interests. Be helpful and knowledgeable when problems arise at work. Help your boss be successful, and he or she might remember you when it's time to promote someone.

If you want to get a promotion, you should make yourself valuable to the company. Take on tasks and projects and complete them well. Make sure your efforts are visible. However, don't brag about your successes. This may cause your bosses and coworkers to dislike you.

Pop-up Questions

1 What might happen if you help your boss be successful?
2 Why should you not brag about your successes?

B **Listen to the conversation and answer the questions.** 09-2

1 Who was promoted to assistant manager?
   a. Patricia   b. Mario   c. Amelia

2 What department does Amelia work in?
   a. Shipping   b. Purchasing   c. Human Resources

3 What does Patricia plan to do?
   a. make an announcement   b. take on more projects   c. become a manager

Vocabulary

A Learn some positions at a company.

	Position	Definition
1	CEO	the chief executive officer of a company; the highest position
2	Accounting Manager	a manager who oversees the Accounting Department
3	Customer Consultant	a staff member who works in the Customer Service Department
4	Staffing Coordinator	a coordinator who organizes and schedules workers and oversees recruiting
5	Board of Directors	an elected group of shareholders who work with the CEO to run the company
6	General Manager	a manager who oversees a company's departments and daily operations
7	File Clerk	an assistant who retrieves and files documents
8	SEO Specialist	a social media expert who works in the Marketing Department

B Look at the hierarchy organizational chart for an advertising agency and fill in the blanks by using the words in A.

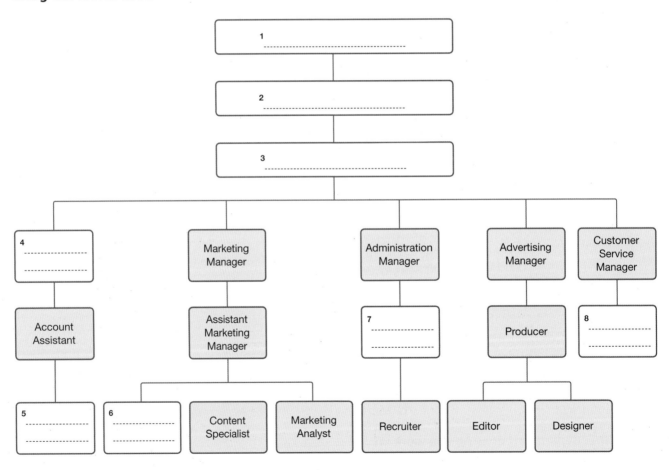

Speak Up

Practice the conversation with your partner by using the information in each announcement. 🔊 09-3

Example

Announcement

A Hi, Tasha. Is this the promotion announcement?

B It is. It was just posted this morning.

A Oh, you got promoted to assistant purchasing manager.

B Yes, I'm very excited to start in April.

A Congratulations. I see Richard Tanaka got promoted.

B Yes, he'll be the new assistant marketing manager starting in August.

A Oh, I see.

B You look disappointed.

A I was hoping for the assistant marketing manager position myself.

B I'm sorry to hear that.

Tips for Success

Offer your congratulations when your coworkers are successful. Offer your condolences when they are not.

A **Let's learn about sense verbs.**

look, feel, smell, sound, or *taste* + adjective (to express your impression of something)	*look, feel, smell, sound,* or *taste* + *like* + noun (to describe something by comparison)
You **look** disappointed. The coffee **smells** delicious. The music in the elevator **sounds** awful. These sandwiches **taste** bland.	He **looks like** his father. The room **smells like** chemicals. Her voice **sounds like** a child's. The cake **tastes like** vanilla.

B **Complete the following sentences by using the correct forms of the verbs in parentheses.**

1 He _____ so depressed. I guess he didn't get the promotion. (look)

2 What happened in here? This room _____ burned toast. (smell)

3 These cookies are delicious! They _____ blueberries. (taste)

4 I think he might be sick. His voice _____ terrible. (sound)

5 We should buy new chairs. These _____ uncomfortable. (feel)

6 Cindy is very fashionable. She _____ a movie star. (look)

7 Joe will speak to the caterer. The food _____ terrible. (taste)

8 I love the new garden. The flowers _____ wonderful. (smell)

Know-how *at* Work   **How to Prepare for an Internal Interview**

Sometimes positions at a company become available. To get promoted, you must do well in an internal interview, also known as a promotion meeting. There are a few ways to prepare for your internal interview.

1 First, talk with your supervisor or manager about your goals. Express your interest in the job and ask for some tips. He or she might even be able to give you a recommendation.

2 Before the interview, research the position. Talk with members of the department about the job expectations. It might even help to ask the person leaving the job for tips.

3 Consider all your skills and make a detailed list. Include all the skills that are relevant to the job. Practice talking about things you've accomplished in your current job. Focus on accomplishments that highlight your skills.

4 Think about all the ways you've improved as an employee. Be prepared to talk about your past mistakes and what you've learned since then.

5 Finally, make a list of questions the hiring committee will ask you. Practice your responses. Ask a friend or a coworker to help you prepare for the interview.

Situation 2

A Cole Newberry talks on the phone with his boss about a problem he solved. Read the telephone conversation. (◁) 09-4

📞 **Jacob Lexington** Hi, Cole. Do you have a minute to chat?

📞 **Cole Newberry** Sure, Mr. Lexington.

📞 **Jacob Lexington** I just wanted to thank you for handling that problem with the supplier.

📞 **Cole Newberry** Oh, no problem at all.

📞 **Jacob Lexington** You showed a lot of initiative. We'd be in deep trouble if you hadn't taken action.

📞 **Cole Newberry** It was really no trouble.

📞 **Jacob Lexington** You interviewed for the assistant production manager job last quarter, right?

📞 **Cole Newberry** That's correct.

📞 **Jacob Lexington** It hasn't been announced yet, but Carla Stone is retiring early next year.

📞 **Cole Newberry** I see. I guess that means Freddy O'Brien will be the new production manager?

📞 **Jacob Lexington** Yes, and the assistant manager job will open again.

📞 **Cole Newberry** Thanks for letting me know.

📞 **Jacob Lexington** I'd like to recommend you for the job.

📞 **Cole Newberry** That's great news.

📞 **Jacob Lexington** You have to pass the interview, of course. And you need to get a good performance review this quarter.

📞 **Cole Newberry** Of course. Thanks again!

Pop-up Questions

1 Why does Mr. Lexington thank Mr. Newberry?
2 Who will retire early next year?
3 What job will open again?
4 What does Mr. Newberry need to get?

B **Problem Solving ::** Cole Newberry must call the Human Resources Department to set up his internal interview. Choose the roles of Cole Newberry and the Human Resources manager. Then, role-play to discuss a possible solution. Use the information from the telephone conversation in A if necessary.

A Let's learn some expressions to use in business.

When asking about availability	When acknowledging effort
Do you have a minute to chat?	We'd be in deep trouble if you hadn't taken action.
Can you spare a few minutes?	All of your hard work really paid off.
Are you available this afternoon?	That was very quick thinking on your part.
Do you have time to visit my office today?	You showed a lot of initiative.
Responding to praise humbly	**When returning praise**
It was really no trouble.	You did a wonderful job as well.
I appreciate your kind words.	I couldn't have done it without you.
I'm just glad it all worked out.	Your support means a lot.

B Fill in the blanks with the correct answers from the box. Then, practice the conversation with a partner. 🔊 09-5

just glad it all worked out	all of your hard work really paid off
can you spare a few minutes	have done it without you

A Hi, Melissa.

B Hi, Jenny. How are you?

A Good. Thank you. ¹_____?

B Sure. What's going on?

A I just wanted to thank you for your help with the website.

B I'm ²_____.

A The new site is looking great now. ³_____.

B I appreciate your kind words. I couldn't ⁴_____.

A Have you thought about interviewing for the supervisor position?

B Yes, I'm very interested.

A I'd like to recommend you for the job.

B That's excellent news. Thank you!

Extra Practice

Role-play with your partner. One person offers some positive feedback. The other person accepts the praise.

A Hi. Do you have a minute to chat?

B Sure. What's going on?

A I wanted to thank you for your help. You showed a lot of initiative.

B It was really no trouble.

Situation 3

Cole Newberry receives an email from the Human Resources manager. Read the email and see if the results are positive or negative.

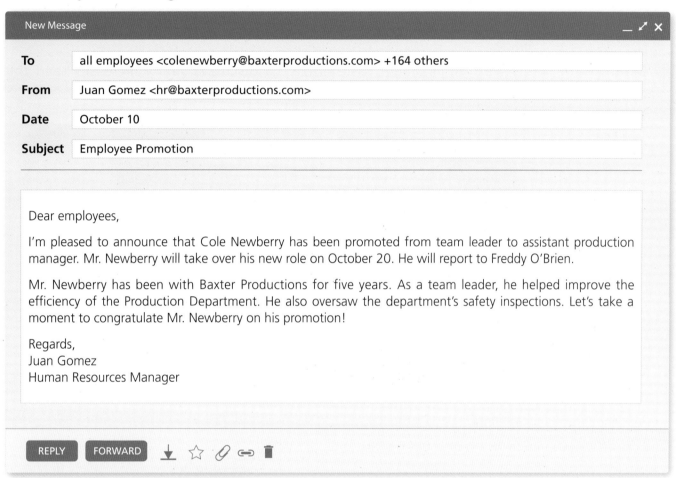

New Message   — ↗ ✕

To	all employees <colenewberry@baxterproductions.com> +164 others
From	Juan Gomez <hr@baxterproductions.com>
Date	October 10
Subject	Employee Promotion

Dear employees,

I'm pleased to announce that Cole Newberry has been promoted from team leader to assistant production manager. Mr. Newberry will take over his new role on October 20. He will report to Freddy O'Brien.

Mr. Newberry has been with Baxter Productions for five years. As a team leader, he helped improve the efficiency of the Production Department. He also oversaw the department's safety inspections. Let's take a moment to congratulate Mr. Newberry on his promotion!

Regards,
Juan Gomez
Human Resources Manager

REPLY   FORWARD   ↓ ☆ 📎 🔗 🗑

Business English Dos and Don'ts

When sending a promotion announcement to a large group of employees, there are a few important things to remember. Include full names as well as job titles to avoid confusion.

Dos
- ○ I'm pleased to announce that Cole Newberry has been promoted. (*includes a full name*)
- ○ Cole Newberry has been promoted from team leader to assistant production manager. (*includes job titles*)

Don'ts
- ✕ I'm delighted to say that Cole has been promoted. (*not specific*)
- ✕ Mr. Newberry will soon work in management. (*not specific*)

Focus on mentioning specific achievements. Don't make vague claims.

Dos
- ○ As a team leader, he helped improve the efficiency of the Production Department. (*specific*)
- ○ He also oversaw the department's safety inspections. (*specific*)

Don'ts
- ✕ As a team leader, he worked very hard. (*too vague*)
- ✕ He also oversaw several important things. (*too vague*)

Situation ❶

Ⓐ Gerard Hunt meets with his manager, Lisa Morris, to discuss a salary increase. Read the conversation. ◀) 10-1

G Thank you for agreeing to meet with me.

L Of course, Mr. Hunt. What would you like to discuss?

G Over the past six months I've performed well in the role of team leader. I've successfully completed several projects, and our sales have increased by 15%. As such, I'd like to discuss my salary.

L I see. You're asking for a raise?

G I've been doing some research. Based on my accomplishments and my years of experience on the marketing team, an increase of 4% is appropriate.

L Unfortunately, that amount is not possible at this time. However, we might revisit the issue in the future.

G So you agree a raise is suitable, but the percentage is not appropriate?

L Yes, I believe so. It's company policy to offer 2.5 to 3% at a time.

G I understand. A raise of 3% is also acceptable. However, I must also ask for an increase in vacation days.

L That seems fair, but I can't guarantee anything yet. Please fill out a salary increase request form. Management will review it within two weeks.

G All right. Thank you for your time.

Pop-up Questions

1 What did Mr. Hunt do over the past year?
2 How much of an increase does Mr. Hunt ask for?
3 Why does Ms. Morris reject Mr. Hunt's proposal?
4 What will Mr. Hunt most likely do next?

B **Take Notes ::** Based on the conversation in A, complete the salary increase request form.

Name	Gerard Hunt	Department	1 _____
Position	2 _____	Rate of Pay Increase	3 _____ %
Achievements	• 4 _____ • 5 _____		

Background Knowledge

A Read and learn about asking for a raise.

Asking for a raise can be an awkward situation. However, it's important to do so, especially if you are not satisfied with your current salary. Before you ask for a raise, consider a few factors. Otherwise, your request might be rejected quickly.

Consider the timing of your request. If the company is doing poorly financially, your request will probably not get approved. Additionally, consider your manager's workload. Your manager might have a lot of stressful situations to handle. In that case, it's not the best time to ask for a raise.

Make sure you are well prepared before you ask for a raise. Research salary trends. Find out what people in your position are usually paid. Then, make a list of your accomplishments. Be prepared to talk about your accomplishments as well as your skills. Finally, decide how much of a raise you will ask for. Set up a meeting with your manager to discuss it.

Pop-up Questions

1 What might happen if your company is doing poorly financially?

2 What should you research before asking for a raise?

B Listen to the conversation and answer the questions. 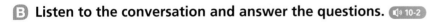 10-2

1 **Who is asking for a raise?**
   a. Mr. Lee   b. Ms. Walker   c. Ms. Tan

2 **What do the man and woman agree on?**
   a. a 2% raise   b. a 3% raise   c. a 4% raise

3 **What does the man tell the woman to do?**
   a. finish a project   b. go to a meeting   c. submit a form

Vocabulary

A **Learn some words related to asking for a raise.**

	Word	Definition
1	salary	the amount of money a worker gets paid annually
2	raise	an increase in salary
3	salary increase request form	a form submitted when an employee wants a raise
4	accomplishment	something positive an employee did, such as completing a project
5	benefit	something given to an employee as part of a contract, such as health insurance
6	performance review	an assessment of an employee's performance at work
7	vacation day	a paid day off work
8	bonus	extra payment given to an employee, usually after a productive year

B **Fill in the blanks with the words in A.**

1 Jennifer won't be here next Friday. She's taking a _____. I think she's going on a trip to Florida for her cousin's wedding. Are you taking any time off this summer?

2 We have a _____ every three months. Our managers assess our skills and leadership qualities. We also get tips on how to improve ourselves.

3 I recently changed jobs. I work for a large international company now. My yearly _____ increased a lot, so I was able to buy a new car.

4 Please fill out a _____. You have to submit it to the Human Resources Department. You also need to submit your most recent performance review.

5 Mark asked for a _____ last month. Our manager agreed to an increase of 5%. Mark must work very hard, so the managers respect him a lot.

6 At the end of every year, the CEO gives each employee a _____. It's an additional payment to say thank you for working hard.

Speak Up

Practice the conversation with your partner by using the information in each form. 🔊 10-3

Example

Name	Hailey Barr	Department	Research and Development
Position	Assistant Manager	Rate of Pay Increase	2.5%

Achievements
- Oversaw product development
- Improved team efficiency

Form 1

Name	Victor Mason	Department	Accounting
Position	Team Leader	Rate of Pay Increase	3.5%

Achievements
- Improved team efficiency
- Trained all new hires

Form 2

Name	Maria Kwon	Department	Operations
Position	Supervisor	Rate of Pay Increase	3%

Achievements
- Increased team productivity
- Improved safety standards

Form 3

Name	Thomas Kirk	Department	Corporate Law
Position	Junior Associate	Rate of Pay Increase	3.8%

Achievements
- Brought on eight new clients
- Won nine of ten cases

A Hello, Ms. Barr. How are things in Research and Development?

B Very good. Thanks for meeting with me.

A Sure. So you'd like to discuss your salary?

B Yes. As a(n) assistant manager, I performed well over the past year.
I oversaw product development and improved team efficiency.

A You've accomplished a lot.

B As such, an increase of 2.5% is appropriate.

A Unfortunately, I'm not sure that's possible right now.

B Is the percentage not acceptable?

A Well, it's company policy to offer 2% at a time.

B That seems fair.

> **! Tips for Success**
>
> When asking for a raise, speak confidently about your accomplishments. Be direct when suggesting percentages and benefits.

A **Let's learn about the present perfect tense.**

Positive	Negative	Interrogative
S + have/has + past participle	S + have/has not (haven't/hasn't) + past participle	Have/Has + S + past participle
You **have accomplished** a lot. She **has performed** very well. I **have been** to Australia.	Mr. Cho **hasn't met** the CEO. I **haven't attended** a conference. The store **hasn't opened** yet.	**Has** Jenny **been** to your office? **Have** you **seen** this movie? **Have** we **finished** the project?

B **Complete the following sentences by using the correct forms of the verbs in parenthesis.**

1 _____ Melanie _____ on her vacation yet? (go)

2 I'm sorry, Mr. Brown. I _____ the report. (not + finish)

3 Sally _____ a lot in her ten years at the company. (accomplish)

4 _____ the boxes _____ delivered? (be)

5 He _____ sick for over two weeks now. (feel)

6 The client _____ the service fee in two months. (not + pay)

7 _____ the receptionist _____ her desk? (leave)

8 I _____ the award three years in a row. (win)

📡 Know-how *at* **Work**   **How to Negotiate a Pay Increase**

Once you ask for a pay increase, you might need to negotiate. Your manager will usually not approve your first request. Thus, you should be prepared to discuss it. There are a few things to remember during negotiations.

1　Never use the words *think*, *believe*, or *might*. These words express uncertainty. Instead, you must show your manager that you are certain you deserve a raise.

2　Before suggesting a percentage, talk about your accomplishments. Speak confidently about your work. Your work benefits the company. List these benefits in clear, concise sentences.

3　Suggest a percentage. Your manager will likely suggest a lower number, so make sure the percentage you suggest is higher than average. But don't suggest a number that is unreasonably high.

4　Sometimes your manager will not offer a satisfactory increase. Instead, ask for some other benefits. This might include flexible work hours or more vacation time.

5　After your meeting, email your manager. Summarize the meeting. This will help your manager remember your agreement.

Situation ②

Ⓐ Gerard Hunt receives an email from the Human Resources Department asking him to fill out a form. Read the email.

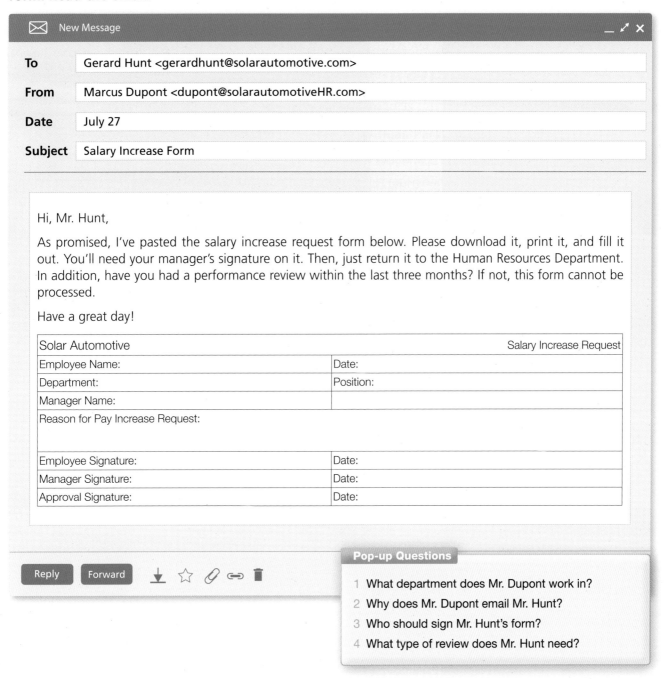

✉ New Message ⎯ ⤢ ✕

To	Gerard Hunt <gerardhunt@solarautomotive.com>
From	Marcus Dupont <dupont@solarautomotiveHR.com>
Date	July 27
Subject	Salary Increase Form

Hi, Mr. Hunt,

As promised, I've pasted the salary increase request form below. Please download it, print it, and fill it out. You'll need your manager's signature on it. Then, just return it to the Human Resources Department. In addition, have you had a performance review within the last three months? If not, this form cannot be processed.

Have a great day!

Solar Automotive		Salary Increase Request
Employee Name:	Date:	
Department:	Position:	
Manager Name:		
Reason for Pay Increase Request:		
Employee Signature:	Date:	
Manager Signature:	Date:	
Approval Signature:	Date:	

Reply Forward ↓ ☆ 📎 🔗 🗑

Pop-up Questions

1 What department does Mr. Dupont work in?
2 Why does Mr. Dupont email Mr. Hunt?
3 Who should sign Mr. Hunt's form?
4 What type of review does Mr. Hunt need?

Ⓑ Problem Solving :: Gerard Hunt did not have a performance review in the last three months. He must call his manager, Lisa Morris, to ask for a review. Choose the roles of Gerard Hunt and Lisa Morris. Then, role-play to discuss a possible solution. Use the information from the email in A if necessary.

Useful Expressions

A Let's learn some expressions to use in business.

When following up after an agreement	When mentioning consequences
As promised, I've pasted the salary increase form below.	If not, this form cannot be processed.
As previously agreed, the rate is now 5%.	Unless it's signed, I can't submit it.
As we discussed, Matt will take over his clients.	If you don't improve, you might receive a warning.
As the contract stated, the deadline is May 3.	Should the file get lost, we have to send it again.

When saying goodbye informally	When responding to an informal goodbye
Have a great day!	You, too!
I appreciate your help.	It's no trouble.
Take care!	Thanks. Have a good one!

B Fill in the blanks with the correct answers from the box. Then, practice the conversation with a partner. ◀》 10-4

> If not, the form can't be processed   Have a great day
> As promised, here's the salary increase request form   You, too

A Hi, Kerry. ¹_____.

B Thanks for dropping it off, Tony.

A No problem. Just fill it out and get your manager's signature on it.

B Okay. Will do.

A You can return it to the Human Resources Department after doing that.

B Okay. Anything else?

A Oh, right. Have you had a performance review in the past three months?

B Hmm. I can't remember when the last one was.

A ²_____.

B I'll ask my manager about it.

A Okay. ³_____!

B ⁴_____!

Extra Practice

Role-play with your partner. One person explains a consequence. The other person responds informally.

A Have you gotten your manager's signature on it?

B No, I haven't.

A Unless it's signed, you can't submit it.

B Thanks for letting me know. Have a great day!

Situation 3

Gerard Hunt receives a voicemail message from Lisa Morris regarding his request. Read the voicemail message and see if the results are positive or negative. 🔊 10-5

You have received one new message sent at 2:35 P.M. on August 11.

Hello, Gerard. This is Lisa Morris calling.

I know you were hoping to get a raise. I'm sorry to say your request was rejected. Unfortunately, it's just not possible at this time. Your performance review was quite good. But as you know, your department struggled a lot last year.

I'm willing to revisit this issue in three months. Pending another good review, you can submit another request. Let me know when you do. I will put in a good word for you with the CEO.

I'm sorry I don't have better news. Thanks for all your hard work regardless. Please call me if you have any further questions.

Business English Dos and Don'ts

When rejecting a valued employee's request, there are a few things to keep in mind.
Acknowledge the employee's request and mention his or her hard work.

Dos	Don'ts
○ I know you were hoping to get a raise. (*acknowledgement*)	✗ Everybody wants a raise these days. (*dismissive*)
○ Your performance review was quite good. (*acknowledgement*)	✗ A good performance review isn't a guarantee. (*dismissive*)

Be apologetic and offer something positive as a consolation.

Dos	Don'ts
○ I'm sorry I don't have better news. (*apologetic*)	✗ This is just the way things are. (*not apologetic*)
○ I will put in a good word for you with the CEO. (*positive*)	✗ I suppose you can try again later if you want. (*not positive enough*)

Being Nominated for an Award

Situation ❶

A Fiona Smith is discussing the year-end party with her coworker, Isaac Conrad. Read the conversation. 🔊 11-1

F Hey, Isaac. Did you get an invitation to the year-end party?

I Not yet. You're planning it, right? When is it?

F That's right. It's on December 28 at 7:00 P.M.

I The same place as last year? I can't remember the name. The Rose Lodge?

F The Rosewood Lodge. Yes, it'll be there again.

I The food was great last year. What sort of entertainment are we having?

F We decided to do something different this year. The CEO will give a speech. Then, we'll have an awards ceremony.

I That sounds similar to what we usually do.

F Yes, but this year we hired a standup comedian. He'll perform for us after dinner.

I That's a great idea. We could all use a good laugh after such a tough year.

F That's true. We're also collecting nominations for the employee of the year award. If you'd like to nominate someone, let me know by December 15.

I Okay. Will do.

F And please RSVP by December 1. Let me know if you're bringing a guest.

Pop-up Questions

1 What did Mr. Conrad not receive yet?
2 Where will the year-end party take place?
3 What will happen after dinner?
4 What is Ms. Smith collecting?

B **Take Notes ::** Based on the conversation in A, complete the invitation.

Wellington Financial Holdiay Party

hosted by [1]_____ (23 Ferguson Lane, Denver, Colorado)

please join us from [2]_____ to 11:00 P.M. on [3]_____

During the evening, you won't want to miss out on a [4]_____ from our CEO, Nigel Keller,

our year-end [5]_____, and [6]_____ comedy performed by Winston Drake.

· Semi-formal attire, please
· RSVP to Fiona Smith by [7]_____
· Nominate your pick for the employee of the year by [8]_____

Background Knowledge

A **Read and learn about selecting the employee of the year.**

Many companies conclude the year with a celebration. This often include an awards ceremony. This ceremony recognizes employees for their hard work. One employee receives the employee of the year award. This award acknowledges the employee's outstanding performance.

Selecting the employee of the year is not always easy. Some companies ask for nominations. Then, they look at each nominee's yearly performance. The employee with the best performance wins the award. In other cases, the CEO or a manager will choose the employee of the year.

Those who become the employee of the year often have similar qualities. They are productive, positive, and enthusiastic about their work. Generally, they work well with others and have good leadership skills. They must also be willing to work hard to achieve the company's goals.

Pop-up Questions

1 What does the year-end celebration often include?

2 Which nominated employee wins the award?

B **Listen to the talk and answer the questions.** 11-2

1 **Who has not RSVPed yet?**

a. Natasha   b. Kirk   c. a guest

2 **What is the man collecting?**

a. invitations   b. nominations   c. menus

3 **How should Natasha send her reply?**

a. by phone   b. in person   c. by email

Vocabulary

A Learn some words related to awards ceremonies.

	Word	Definition
1	awards ceremony	an event at which awards are presented to honor achievements
2	nominate	to suggest someone for an award
3	nominee	a person who has been suggested for an award
4	employee of the year	an award recognizing the best employee in a company
5	acceptance speech	a speech given by a winner after an award is presented
6	invitation	a card or an email that requests someone attend an event
7	RSVP	an acronym that asks someone to reply to an invitation; to reply to an invitation
8	entertainment	music, performances, etc.

B Fill in the blanks with the words in A.

1 I received a(n) _____ to her retirement party. However, the party is on Saturday, and I already have plans. I don't think I can attend it. Are you planning on going?

2 He's a sales representative at the company. Did you know he was chosen as the _____ three years in a row? I think he deserves a promotion for his hard work.

3 Please _____ by April 12. Make sure to indicate how many guests you are bringing as well. That way, we can order enough food and beverages for everyone.

4 Who will you _____ for the outstanding leadership award? I think Kevin deserves it this year. He's always solving problems, and he's a great role model for new employees.

5 The _____ was at the Alliance Hotel last year, right? Where will we have it this year? I hope there's a buffet and entertainment.

6 Cindy, you've been chosen as the employee of the year. You'll receive the award at the year-end party. You have to give a(n) _____ at the party.

Speak Up

Practice the conversation with your partner by using the information in the invitations. 11-3

Example

You're invited to the

Bold Media Year-End Party

hosted by

The Infinity Hotel
4 Houghten Avenue
Sydney, New South Wales

please join us from 8:00 to 11:30 P.M.
on December 29

During the evening, you won't want to miss out on a speech from our founder, Kelly Bold, our year-end awards ceremony, and music performed by the Jazz Kings.

| Semi-formal attire, please | RSVP to Marshall Price by December 10 | Nominate your pick for the employee of the year by December 13 |

Invitation

You're invited to the

Trident Holiday Party

hosted by

The Brook Lodge
32 King Street
Toronto, Ontario

please join us from 7:30 to 11:00 P.M.
on December 27

During the evening, you won't want to miss out on a speech from our CEO, Ben Jones, our year-end awards ceremony, and standup comedy performed by Willy Kim.

| Semi-formal attire, please | RSVP to Leon Peterson by December 3 | Nominate your pick for the employee of the year by December 8 |

A Hello, Sammy. Here's your invitation to the year-end party.

B Thanks, Marshall. I see it's at the Infinity Hotel again.

A That's right. It's on December 29 at 8:00 P.M.

B Oh, and there will be music as well?

A We hired the Jazz Kings this year. They're/He's amazing.

B Wow, it sounds even better than last year's party.

A I hope so. Just make sure you RSVP by December 10.
   And let me know how many guests you're bringing.

B No problem.

A You can also nominate someone for the employee of the year award.
   Let me know your pick by December 13.

> **! Tips for Success**
>
> When delivering an invitation in person, make sure to emphasize the RSVP date and any other relevant dates.

A Let's learn about the modal verb *can*.

ability	permission
He **can** speak four languages. She **can** dance very well.	You **can** use this conference room. He **can** take the day off tomorrow.
request	**offer**
Can you close the window? **Can** you meet the client now?	I **can** help with the project. We **can** do the presentation.
possibility	**not allowed**
It **can** get very hot there in summer. Driving at night **can** be dangerous.	You **cannot** bring food into this room. We **can't** go home early today.

B Fill in the blanks with the words in the box. Add *can* or *can't* to each sentence.

succeed	turn on	contact	attend	come	fly	speak	use

1 _____ Tim _____ the client to set up a meeting?

2 You _____ the air conditioner. It's still broken.

3 With some hard work, anyone _____ at this job.

4 Cindy, _____ I _____ your phone for a minute?

5 Mr. Jones _____ English, French, and Chinese.

6 Richard, _____ you _____ to my office?

7 You _____ the gala with us if you like.

8 They _____ to Chicago. It's snowing too heavily.

Know-how *at* **Work**   How to Prepare for a Speech

When you receive a work award, you might have to give a speech. Many people get nervous when speaking in front of a crowd, especially in front of their coworkers. There are a few things you can do to prepare.

1 Coming up with a speech on the spot is usually not a good idea. You may forget to thank certain people. Your thoughts might also seem disorganized. Instead, you should write your speech in advance.

2 It's important that your speech be entertaining but humble, so edit your speech a few times. Show your speech to some of your coworkers. Ask for feedback and apply it.

3 Use the resources available to you. Many websites provide excellent tips for giving a great speech. Your Human Resources Department might also have some tips to offer.

4 Memorize your speech. Practice it in front of a mirror. Make sure your body language is relaxed and remember to smile. Don't speak too fast and pause for applause or laughter.

Situation ②

A Fiona Smith receives an email from her manager about the employee of the year award. Read the email.

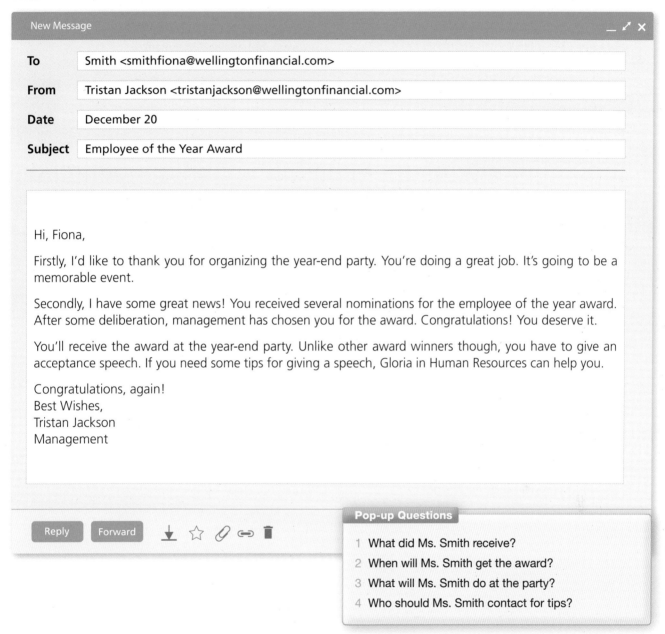

New Message   _ ↗ ✕

To	Smith <smithfiona@wellingtonfinancial.com>
From	Tristan Jackson <tristanjackson@wellingtonfinancial.com>
Date	December 20
Subject	Employee of the Year Award

Hi, Fiona,

Firstly, I'd like to thank you for organizing the year-end party. You're doing a great job. It's going to be a memorable event.

Secondly, I have some great news! You received several nominations for the employee of the year award. After some deliberation, management has chosen you for the award. Congratulations! You deserve it.

You'll receive the award at the year-end party. Unlike other award winners though, you have to give an acceptance speech. If you need some tips for giving a speech, Gloria in Human Resources can help you.

Congratulations, again!
Best Wishes,
Tristan Jackson
Management

Reply   Forward   ↓ ☆ ⬗ ⌒ 🗑

Pop-up Questions

1 What did Ms. Smith receive?

2 When will Ms. Smith get the award?

3 What will Ms. Smith do at the party?

4 Who should Ms. Smith contact for tips?

B **Problem Solving ::** Fiona Smith has never given a speech before. She must contact Gloria in Human Resources for tips. Find a partner and choose the roles of Fiona Smith and Gloria. Then, role-play to discuss a possible solution. Use the information from the email in A if necessary.

Useful Expressions

A Let's learn some expressions to use in business.

When providing advice	When expressing anticipation
If you need some tips, Gloria can help you.	It's going to be a memorable event.
You should ask Mark in Human Resources for help.	I can't wait for the year-end party.
It's probably best to practice the speech in advance.	I'm so excited to see him perform.
It would be best if you attended the ceremony.	I'm really looking forward to the trip.
When offering congratulations to a winner	**When responding to congratulations**
Congratulations!	Thank you!
You deserve it!	It's such an honor.
Let me be the first to congratulate you!	Thank you. I appreciate it.

B Fill in the blanks with the correct answers from the box. Then, practice the conversation with a partner. ◀)) 11-4

> I'm really looking forward to it   Congratulations
> If you need some tips, Tammy can help you   It's such an honor

A Hi, Jeffrey. Thanks so much for planning the holiday party.

B Oh, it was no trouble.

A You did a great job. ¹_____.

B Me, too.

A I have some good news. You've been chosen as the employee of the year.

B Wow, that's incredible.

A ²_____! You really deserve it.

B Thank you. ³_____!

A You have to give an acceptance speech at the party.

B Oh, I see. I've never given a speech before.

A Don't worry. ⁴_____.

Extra Practice

Role-play with your partner. One person makes an announcement. The other person accepts the congratulations.

A You've been chosen as Leader of the Year.

B Wow, that's incredible.

A Let me be the first to congratulate you!

B Thank you. I appreciate it.

Situation 3

Fiona Smith gives an acceptance speech at the year-end party. Read the speech and see if the results are positive or negative. ◀» 11-5

Nigel Keller

Finally, I'm very pleased to present the award for the employee of the year. This year's winner has shown outstanding commitment to Wellington Financial's core values. Let's all give Fiona Smith a big round of applause!

Fiona Smith

Thank you, Mr. Keller. It's truly an honor to receive this award. It's also an honor to be nominated from among so many fantastic people.

I would not be up here without the support of my team and my managers. I thank you all for helping me get to where I am today. I'll never forget my first day at the office. So many of you were kind and patient. Since then, you have helped me learn and grow as an employee.

It has been five years, and I'm happy to call Wellington Financial home. I'm proud to be part of such a wonderful group. I promise to keep working hard and to keep improving. Thank you.

Business English Dos and Don'ts

When accepting an award, there are a few things to consider. Recognize the hard work of others. Do not focus only on your own accomplishments.

Dos	Don'ts
○ It's also an honor to be nominated from among so many fantastic people. (*grateful*)	✗ Management made the best choice in the end. (*arrogant*)
○ I would not be up here without the support of my team and my managers. (*grateful*)	✗ I suppose I should thank my coworkers. (*too reluctant*)

Express your gratitude toward the company as a whole.

Dos	Don'ts
○ I'm happy to call Wellington Financial home. (*grateful*)	✗ I've enjoyed some aspects of working here. (*too blunt*)
○ I'm proud to be part of such a wonderful group. (*grateful*)	✗ I've put a lot of work into this company. (*ungrateful*)

Situation ❶

Ⓐ **Annika Stone is discussing her retirement with her company's CEO, Elton Adams. Read the conversation.** 🔊 12-1

A Hi, Mr. Adams. Thanks for meeting with me.

E No problem. I understand you want to discuss your retirement.

A Yes. I've been at the company for twenty years now. I know retirement age is 65, but I'd like to retire a few years early. I want to spend more time with my grandchildren.

E I understand. You've been a great asset to this company. Can I encourage you to stay on for six more months?

A Well, I was planning to leave in March. However, I could stay until May if need be.

E That would be very helpful. As you know, the Human Resources Department is currently understaffed. I'd appreciate it if you could lend a hand in looking for a replacement.

A Sure. I might have a few colleagues to recommend.

E Great. We need someone to start in April. That way, you will have ample time to train your replacement.

A That sounds fair.

E You should also introduce your replacement to your clients.

A Of course. That won't be a problem at all.

Pop-up Questions

1 Why does Ms. Stone want to retire?

2 What month did Ms. Stone plan to leave?

3 What does Mr. Adams say about Human Resources?

4 When should the replacement start?

B **Take Notes** :: Based on the conversation in A, complete the CEO's to do list.

TO DO:

- Find a replacement by [1]_____ – Annika will [2]_____
- Train [3]_____ – [4]_____ will handle this
- Introduce the replacement to Annika's [5]_____ – Annika will handle this
- Plan a retirement party for Annika – Annika will reitre in [6]_____

Background Knowledge

A **Read and learn about giving notice when resigning.**

Leaving a job can be an uncomfortable situation. Whether you want to retire, take a few years off, or find a new job, you should give your employer notice. There are a few things to remember when doing so.

It's standard practice to give two weeks' notice. This means you will leave your job two weeks after your announcement. In that time, your employer may ask you to help with the transition. This might mean training your replacement. It might also mean teaching your coworkers about your projects.

Some employment contracts indicate a longer period of notice. In this case, follow your contract. Meet with your employer and announce your resignation. Your employer might also ask you for a written resignation letter. Being polite and helpful during the process can go a long way. After all, you may need to ask your employer for a reference if you want to get another job.

Pop-up Questions

1 What does two weeks' notice mean?
2 What might your employer ask you to submit?

B **Listen to the conversation and answer the questions.** 🔊 12-2

1 **Who is resigning from the company?**
   a. Ms. Kim   b. Mr. Bell   c. Mr. Benson

2 **Why is the man moving overseas?**
   a. to start a new job   b. to attend university   c. to be with his family

3 **What department will the man likely contact next?**
   a. Sales   b. Human Resources   c. Accounting

Vocabulary

A Learn some words related to resigning.

resignation letter

replacement

employment contract

reference / recommendation

get fired

resign

introduce

retirement party

B Choose the correct answer for each blank.

1 Margo will retire in June, so let's have a(n) _____.

   a. introduce   b. replacement   c. reference   d. retirement party

2 Let me _____ you to our sales manager. This is Mr. Blake.

   a. resign   b. introduce   c. replacement   d. resignation letter

3 We need to find a(n) _____. Can you post a job advertisement?

   a. replacement   b. get fired   c. recommendation   d. introduce

4 Please read your _____. There are rules regarding resignations.

   a. introduce   b. resign   c. get fired   d. employment contract

5 I heard he _____. He's looking for a new job now.

   a. got fired   b. reference

   c. retirement party   d. replacement

6 Try to be cooperative when leaving a job.
You might need a _____ in the future.

   a. replacement   b. retirement party

   c. resignation letter   d. recommendation

Speak Up

Practice the conversation with your partner by using the information on each to-do list. 🔊 12-3

Example

- Find a replacement by June
  (Tim will recommend a few colleagues)
- Train the replacement – how to lead sales meetings
- Introduce the replacement to Tim's clients
- Plan a retirement party for Tim
  (sometime in July)

To-Do List 1

- Find a replacement by September
  (Denise will post a job advertisement)
- Train the replacement – how to manage purchase orders
- Introduce the replacement to our suppliers
- Plan a retirement party for Denise
  (sometime in October)

To-Do List 2

- Find a replacement by January
  (Karen will promote an intern)
- Train the replacement – how to answer the phones
- Teach the replacement our filing system
- Plan a retirement party for Karen
  (sometime in February)

To-Do List 3

- Find a replacement by March
  (George will promote someone)
- Train the replacement – how to draft budget reports
- Introduce the replacement to our overseas branch
- Plan a retirement party for George
  (sometime in April)

A Hi, Tim. I heard you want to discuss your retirement.

B Yes. I'm going to retire in June.

A Can I encourage you to stay on for another three months?

B Hmm. I could stay until the end of July.

A Okay. Can you help find a replacement by June?

B Sure. I'll recommend a few colleagues.

A You should also train the replacement.

   You should teach him or her how to lead sales meetings.

B That makes sense. I'll introduce the replacement to my clients, too.

A I'd also like to plan a retirement party for you. Sometime in July.

B That would be wonderful.

! Tips for Success

When retiring from a career, be prepared for management to ask you for help during the transition.

GRAMMAR

A **Let's learn about to-infinitives as object complements.**

A to-infinitive can express the desired or intended action of the object.	
positive	interrogative
I expect him to agree to the proposal. The manager allowed us to attend the meeting. We really want him to join our team. They forced us to close our business.	Can I encourage you to stay on for another three months? Can you ask Ms. Baker to stop by my office? Can we persuade him to sign the contract?

B **Fill in the blanks with the words in the box. Add _to_ before each verb.**

buy answer behave meet change email pay ask

1 Anna told Steve _____ the phones at the front desk.

2 Can we force the customer _____ the fee?

3 The CEO expects all employees _____ appropriately.

4 Mr. Walker encouraged me _____ for a raise.

5 Can I persuade you _____ the client tomorrow?

6 I want the company _____ its refund policy.

7 The raise enabled me _____ a new house.

8 I need him _____ the client.

Know-how _at_ Work   How to Leave A Job

It's important to stay organized once you decide to leave your job. There are many issues you will have to handle. There are a few ways you can ensure you don't forget anything.

1   The first step is to give two weeks' notice. Submit your resignation letter. After that, make a list of things you need to do.

2   Figure out when you will get your final paycheck. Different companies have different rules. You might get paid on your regular payday. Or you might get paid on your last day of work.

3   Find out if you have any unused time off. This includes vacation days as well as sick days. Your company will often pay you for these unused days.

4   Ask for references. This is important if you plan to get another job. Be cooperative, and your managers will likely give you positive references.

5   Determine if you can receive benefits. In some cases, you can still receive benefits, such as health insurance, for a period of time after you leave your job.

Situation ②

A Annika Stone gets a text message from her boss asking how her replacement is doing. Read the text message chain.

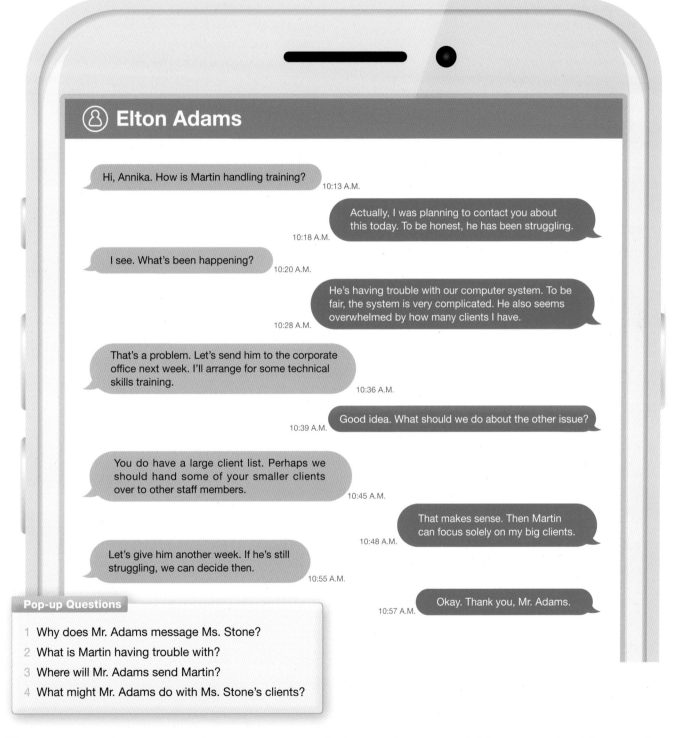

Elton Adams

Hi, Annika. How is Martin handling training?
10:13 A.M.

Actually, I was planning to contact you about this today. To be honest, he has been struggling.
10:18 A.M.

I see. What's been happening?
10:20 A.M.

He's having trouble with our computer system. To be fair, the system is very complicated. He also seems overwhelmed by how many clients I have.
10:28 A.M.

That's a problem. Let's send him to the corporate office next week. I'll arrange for some technical skills training.
10:36 A.M.

Good idea. What should we do about the other issue?
10:39 A.M.

You do have a large client list. Perhaps we should hand some of your smaller clients over to other staff members.
10:45 A.M.

That makes sense. Then Martin can focus solely on my big clients.
10:48 A.M.

Let's give him another week. If he's still struggling, we can decide then.
10:55 A.M.

Okay. Thank you, Mr. Adams.
10:57 A.M.

Pop-up Questions

1 Why does Mr. Adams message Ms. Stone?
2 What is Martin having trouble with?
3 Where will Mr. Adams send Martin?
4 What might Mr. Adams do with Ms. Stone's clients?

B **Problem Solving ::** Annika Stone must call Elton Adams to ask him to reschedule Martin's training session as Martin is taking a sick day. Find a partner and choose the roles of Annika Stone and Elton Adams. Then, role-play to discuss a possible solution. Use the information from the text message chain in A if necessary.

 **Useful Expressions**

A Let's learn some expressions to use in business.

When asking for more information about a problem	When making a concession
What's been happening?	To be fair, the system is very complicated.
What sort of problems?	Granted, there have been many problems.
What's going on?	You do have a large client list.
Can you elaborate on that?	Understandably, it is a lot to handle.
When expressing understanding	**When expressing confusion**
That makes sense.	I'm sorry, but I'm confused.
That's understandable.	I'm not sure I understand.
That's a fair assessment.	That doesn't quite make sense.

B Fill in the blanks with the correct answers from the box. Then, practice the conversation with a partner. 🔊 12-4

I'm not sure I understand	What sort of problems
Understandably, it is a lot to handle	That makes sense

A Hi, Xander. How is Ellen handling training?

B To be honest, there have been some problems.

A ¹ _____?

B Well, she has had trouble with my clients.

A ² _____.

B Oh. Well, it's just that she's not sure how to manage all of them.

A ³ _____.

B You're right. I do have a pretty large client list.

A Let's give her a few weeks. She might improve by then.

B ⁴ _____.

A Let me know if there are any other issues.

Extra Practice

Role-play with your partner. A CEO asks about a trainee's progress. The trainer gives an update.

A What's been happening?

B Henry has had trouble with our computer system.

A To be fair, the system is very complicated.

B That's true. Let's give him another week.

Situation 3

Annika Stone gets a voicemail from the CEO inviting her to her retirement party. Read the voicemail and see if the results are positive or negative. 🔊 12-5

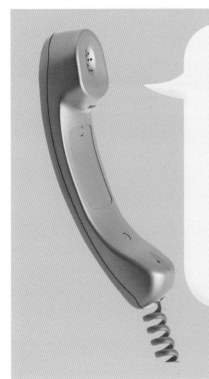

You have one new message sent at 9:35 A.M. on May 28.

Hi, Annika. This is Elton calling. I wanted to thank you for staying on a few extra weeks. Thanks to you, Martin is now ready to handle most of your clients. I appreciate all the work you did to prepare him.

Next week, we're going to have your retirement party at the Surfside Grill. I heard you love seafood, so I asked Jane to book us the party room. Your department as well as the management staff will be there. It's a Friday, so we're going to leave work early. Our reservation is for 4:30 P.M. You can carpool with Jane to the restaurant if you like.

Thanks again, Annika!

Business English Dos and Don'ts

When inviting a colleague to a party, there are a few important things to consider. Mention the purpose of the party and who will attend. Try not to be vague about the occasion unless it is a surprise party.

Dos

○ Next week, we're going to have your retirement party. (*mentions occasion*)

○ Your department as well as the management staff will be there. (*mentions attendees*)

Don'ts

✗ On Friday, we're going to have a party. (*not specific*)

✗ Several of us will be there. (*not specific*)

Be clear about the time. Provide directions or a way to get to the event.

Dos

○ Our reservation is for 4:30 P.M. (*clear*)

○ You can carpool with Jane to the restaurant. (*clear*)

Don'ts

✗ Be there early in the evening. (*vague*)

✗ Ask someone for a ride. (*vague*)

Answer Key

Mission 01 Recruiting New Employees

Situation ❶

A

1 She works in the Human Resources Department.
2 It has a lot of new clients.
3 Ms. Ellis will place some job advertisements.
4 She will go to Richmond University's job fair.

B

1 maintain good client relationships
2 two years of experience in a sales position
3 Janette Ellis
4 April 20
5 mid-May

Background Knowledge

A

1 You might be able to fill a position by promoting someone.
2 They will submit applications and résumés.

B

> W Jeff, this is Margo calling. As you know, we're going to open another restaurant downtown. But we need to hire a head chef.
> M Would you like me to post some job advertisements?
> W That might help. However, I wonder if there are any job fairs coming up.
> M Actually, the Westmount Culinary School is having a job fair next month.
> W That's great. Could you and Theresa in Human Resources attend it?
> M Sure. I'll call Theresa today and set everything up.

1 c 　　　　　　 2 a 　　　　　　 3 b

Vocabulary

1 Personal Summary
2 Experience
3 Education
4 Post-secondary Institution
5 Skills
6 References

GRAMMAR

1 at 　　　　　　 2 on
3 during 　　　　 4 until
5 in 　　　　　　 6 for
7 on 　　　　　　 8 in

Situation ❷

A

1 Janette Ellis recommended her for the position.
2 She used to work at Sandford Labs.
3 She moved to L.A. to be closer to her family.
4 She wants a permanent full-time position.

Useful Expressions

1 Peter Umber spoke very highly of you
2 worked at Umber Securities for three years
3 I see you were also employed at Kent Investment
4 I think you'll do a great job here

Mission 02 Welcoming New Employees

Situation ❶

A

1 It recently finished its spring hiring period.
2 He will give the opening speech.
3 It will happen on May 9.
4 She will call the caterer.

B

1 Opening
2 CEO
3 Tour
4 Cafeteria
5 department managers

Background Knowledge

A

1 It often details the history and culture of the company.
2 They head to their respective departments to learn more about their jobs.

B

W Hello, everyone. Please take a seat. I'm Priya Tasmir, the manager of the Research and Development Department. I hope you enjoyed the tour of our facilities as well as the catered lunch. We're going to spend the afternoon here in the lab, where you'll continue your training. As you know, the lab equipment can be very dangerous. So please pay careful attention to the safety demonstration. Before we start, please put on your safety helmet. Then, come and pick up your ID card. I'll let you know your assigned passcodes as well. You'll need them to get in and out of the lab.

1 b　　　　　　　**2** a　　　　　　　**3** c

Vocabulary

B

1 CEO
2 guide
3 take a tour
4 receive an ID card
5 trainer
6 introduce myself
7 listen to his speech
8 watch a training video

GRAMMAR

1 doing	2 Does	3 do
4 Did	5 Do	6 does
7 Did	8 doing	

Situation ❷

A

1 He is attending a conference.
2 He has to attend several more meetings.
3 He will return on May 11.
4 She asks him to let her know if the orientation session can be delayed.

Useful Expressions

1 As you're aware
2 I understand you've put a lot of effort into
3 my team worked very hard
4 understands if it's too late to reschedule

Situation ❶

A

1 She wants to attract new customers.
2 She asks him to put together a customer satisfaction survey.
3 It specializes in delivering prepackaged meals.
4 It recently launched an app.

B

1 satisfaction	2 quality
3 packaging	4 speed
5 website	6 service hotline
7 damaged	

Background Knowledge

A

1 Surveys help companies change or develop new policies.
2 Online surveys are the most widely used method.

B

M Hi, Katherine. Since we're approaching the end of the year, we should get some customer feedback.

W Certainly. How about an online survey?

M That works. Please include questions about our customer service, product pricing, and refund policy.

W Okay. Got it.

M I think Melinda made the survey last year. You can ask her for tips.

W Okay. I'll give her a call.

M We should start collecting data next Friday, so let me know if there are any problems.

W Thanks, Arthur.

1 a　　　　　　　**2** b　　　　　　　**3** b

Vocabulary

1 packaging	2 billing accuracy
3 customer service	4 delivery speed

GRAMMAR

1 why he was fired from his last job
2 where I can submit my application form
3 when the company picnic is

4 what the company's policy is

5 how the orientation session was

6 where the new office is

7 what the application deadline is

8 why he was upset this afternoon

Situation ❷

Ⓐ

1 She works for Fresh Connect Meals.

2 They will get a discount code for 10% off their next order.

3 It asks about the speed of delivery.

4 It asks if the app is easier to use than the website.

Useful Expressions

1 I would be grateful if you provided

2 how often do you shop at

3 which is easier to use, our app or website

4 Go to our website

Mission 04 | Getting an Overseas Assignment

Situation ❶

Ⓐ

1 It will open in Berlin, Germany.

2 Two positions will open.

3 It is 10 months long.

4 They are due on April 3.

Ⓑ

1 Berlin, Germany   2 April 3

3 Chemical Engineer   4 Human Resources

5 10   6 language training

Background Knowledge

Ⓐ

1 There are three types of international assignment.

2 They should learn about the country and its culture before going on an international assignment.

Ⓑ

M Hi, Karen. Did you see the company notice?

W Hey, Rob. Do you mean the one for the international assignment?

M Yeah, that one. It looks great. Living in Paris sounds incredible.

W It does. Are you going to apply?

M Well, the position calls for three years of experience. I only have two.

W Right. I'm planning to apply. I'm just worried about the duration of the job.

M How long is it for?

W It's a long-term assignment so around two years. I'm worried about experiencing culture shock.

M You could take some culture training first. Ask Marina. I think she worked in Russia a few years ago.

1 a   2 a   3 c

Vocabulary

Ⓑ

1 b   2 c   3 h

4 g   5 f   6 a

7 e   8 d

GRAMMAR

1 few

2 boxes

3 much/lots of/a lot of

4 a little

5 lots of/a lot of

6 many/lots of/a lot of

7 chairs

8 some

Situation ❷

Ⓐ

1 She emails him to tell him that he was selected for an interview.

2 It's on April 27 at 10:30 A.M.

3 It will take place in room 12B on the third floor.

4 She asks if any of his family members will accompany him.

Useful Expressions

1 I'm happy to let you know that you were chosen

2 Thank you for informing me

3 will take place at 10:00 A.M. on Monday

4 Please come to the Human Resources Department

Mission 05 — Planning a Charity Event

Situation ❶

A

1 The CEO asked her to plan it.
2 A live auction will take place.
3 It will take place in March.
4 Rick will reach out to local donors.

B

1 live auction   2 mid-March
3 Art Gallery   4 auctioneer
5 Reach out to   6 Set up
7 cleanup

Background Knowledge

A

1 First, you should pick a cause.
2 You should hire an event planner.

B

> W Hi, Deepak. This is Faridah calling. We're going to host a walkathon to raise money for cancer research. We held this event last year, and it was very successful. However, Trisha is on maternity leave, so I'd like you to plan it instead. The event will be at Hyde Park on April 25. You need to send registration forms to everyone at the company. Each employee will collect donations and then participate in the walk. Prior to the event, we need to make event T-shirts. The company will cover the cost. We'll also serve beverages at the event. Please call me back if you have any questions. Thank you!

1 a   2 a   3 b

Vocabulary

B

1 live auction   2 concert
3 sporting event   4 fair
5 art exhibit   6 online auction
7 fun run   8 silent auction

GRAMMAR

1 to let   2 to accept
3 to eat   4 to look
5 to get   6 to ask
7 to relax   8 to change

Situation ❷

A

1 It's on March 15.
2 Garrison Media is hosting a charity concert.
3 He is worried attendance will be low.
4 He recommends postponing the auction.

Useful Expressions

1 Could I get your opinion on something
2 I think it's best to postpone the concert
3 I don't think we can do that
4 However, I'm worried attendance will be low

Mission 06 — Dealing with Complaints

Situation ❶

A

1 She writes that the update messed everything up.
2 She can add ten items.
3 It freezes and closes without warning.
4 She hopes the app is fixed soon.

B

1 deleted
2 replied to
3 international
4 payment information

Background Knowledge

A

1 It helps companies identify problems.
2 They can provide a wide variety of feedback about products and services.

B

> W Hi, Leon. This is Natalie calling. I've been reading reviews of our app. It seems our customers are experiencing a lot of problems. Several of them mentioned the wish list doesn't work. It's impossible to save items. A few others also complained about our shipping options. There's no way to track shipments. Additionally, the last update made things worse. The app now freezes and closes frequently. I'm going to email you my full report. I'd like you to meet with Denise in IT to discuss this as soon as possible.

1 a   2 b   3 c

Vocabulary

Ⓑ

1 b	2 c	3 d
4 a	5 d	6 b

GRAMMAR

1 has been working
2 has been discussing
3 have been traveling
4 has not / hasn't been answering
5 have been thinking
6 has not / hasn't been reading
7 has not / hasn't been washing
8 has been watching

Situation ❷

Ⓐ

1 She will handle the problem with the wish lists.
2 He says there are no international shipping options.
3 The customers' preferred payment options disappear.
4 He will draft an announcement.

Useful Expressions

1 Thank you for joining me
2 I'll fix that
3 I'd like you to work on that
4 I'll start right away

Mission 07 Preparing for a Sales Meeting

Situation ❶

Ⓐ

1 It will start with a speech from the regional sales manager.
2 He is on medical leave.
3 He should compare the yearly sales figures with last year's figures.
4 He should post it in the Sales Department.

Ⓑ

1 Sales Department
2 Sales Meeting
3 January 11
4 theater

5 10:00 A.M.
6 a speech
7 yearly in-store and online sales
8 catered lunch

Background Knowledge

Ⓐ

1 A manager or a company executive usually leads the meeting.
2 Having too many sales meetings can decrease employee productivity.

Ⓑ

> M Hi, Olga. This is Jeremiah calling. Dennis is on medical leave, so I'd like you to plan our monthly sales meeting. I will send you our monthly sales figures by email. Please compare them to last month. In addition, make note of any trends over the last sixth months. The meeting will be on October 2 at 11:00 A.M. I've already reserved conference room 306. Please post a memo in the Sales Department. Be sure to mention that there will be a catered lunch in the cafeteria after.

1 a	2 b	3 c

Vocabulary

Ⓑ

1 c	2 a	3 d
4 d	5 b	6 a

GRAMMAR

1 made	2 took	3 gave
4 make	5 take	6 make
7 take	8 give	

Situation ❷

Ⓐ

1 He is discussing online sales.
2 Baby and children's clothing sales increased.
3 The in-store sales remained the same.
4 She compiled a list of common customer complaints.

Useful Expressions

1 Let's move on to international sales
2 This chart shows our profits from
3 Exports dropped significantly in the summer
4 Our customers are obviously unhappy

Mission 08 — Moving to a New Office

Situation ❶

A

1 It was very successful.
2 The company will move on February 2.
3 They should clean up their workspaces.
4 Someone in customer service should send it.

B

1 Newcastle
2 February 2
3 January 28
4 personal items
5 electrical equipment
6 Notify customers
7 January 20

Background Knowledge

A

1 Expansion is the most common reason.
2 It might not be able to renew an expensive lease.

B

> W   Hello, department managers. As you're aware, our sales numbers were not great last year. We had to let a few employees go. Because of this, our office space is much too large. So we're going to merge our office with another office downtown. The move is set for March 10. Prior to that, I need you to post a notice in your departments. Please ask all employees to clean up their workspaces by March 5. They must pack up their personal items on March 9. I need someone to update our website as well. We should post the new address and a map of the area.

1 a
2 b
3 a

Vocabulary

B

1 d
2 f
3 a
4 e
5 b
6 c
7 h
8 g

GRAMMAR

1 must finish
2 don't have to work
3 has to go
4 must not leave
5 must speak
6 doesn't have to redo
7 must apologize
8 have to turn

Situation ❷

A

1 He works for Ashmore Renovations.
2 There is a lot of water damage.
3 They will take at least three weeks.
4 The building owner will cover the cost of the repairs.

Useful Expressions

1 I have some unfortunate news to share
2 That's disappointing
3 Do you think it will take longer
4 That puts our earliest moving date at

Mission 09 — Getting a Promotion

Situation ❶

A

1 Ms. Aman is the new marketing manager.
2 He was hoping to get a promotion.
3 He will retire in April.
4 She will check her email.

B

1 marketing
2 shipping
3 May
4 assistant production

Background Knowledge

A

1 He or she might remember you when it's time to promote someone.
2 Your bosses and coworkers may dislike you.

B

> M   Hi, Patricia. Did you see the announcement?
> W   Hi, Mario. You mean the one listing the promotions? I saw you got promoted to assistant manager. Congratulations!
> M   Thanks! Amelia in Human Resources was also promoted.
> W   I saw that. I'm happy for her.

M But you look disappointed.

W Well, I was hoping to get promoted, too.

M Oh, I see. Maybe next time.

W Yes, I'm going to take on more projects this year.

M I'm sure your manager will recommend you for a promotion then.

1 b   **2** c   **3** b

Vocabulary

1 CEO

2 Board of Directors

3 General Manager

4 Accounting Manager

5 File Clerk

6 SEO Specialist

7 Staffing Coordinator

8 Customer Consultant

GRAMMAR

1 looks   **2** smells like

3 taste like   **4** sounds

5 feel   **6** looks like

7 tastes   **8** smell

Situation ❷

Ⓐ

1 Mr. Newberry handled a problem with a supplier.

2 Carla Stone will retire early next year.

3 The assistant manager job will open again.

4 He needs to get a good performance review.

Useful Expressions

1 Can you spare a few minutes

2 just glad it all worked out

3 All of your hard work really paid off

4 have done it without you

Situation ❶

Ⓐ

1 He performed well in the role of team leader.

2 He asks for a 4% increase.

3 The percentage is not appropriate.

4 He will fill out a salary increase request form.

Ⓑ

1 Team Leader

2 Marketing Department

3 3

4 Successfully completed several projects

5 Sales have increased by 15%

Background Knowledge

Ⓐ

1 Your request will probably not get approved.

2 You should research salary trends.

Ⓑ

W Hello, Mr. Lee. Thank you for agreeing to meet with me.

M Of course, Ms. Walker. So you want to discuss your salary?

W Yes. I've performed well as the assistant marketing manager over the past year. My team has successfully completed many projects. As such, a 3% raise is appropriate.

M Unfortunately, we can only offer 2% at this time.

W That's acceptable.

M All right. Fill out a salary increase form. Then, submit it to Ms. Tan in Human Resources.

1 b   **2** a   **3** c

Vocabulary

Ⓑ

1 vacation day

2 performance review

3 salary

4 salary increase request form

5 raise

6 bonus

GRAMMAR

1 Has/gone

2 haven't finished

3 has accomplished

4 Have/been

5 has felt

6 hasn't paid

7 Has/left

8 have won

Situation ❷

1 He works in the Human Resources Department.

2 He emails him to send a salary increase request form.

3 His manager should sign his form.

4 He needs a performance review.

Useful Expressions

1 As promised, here's the salary increase request form

2 If not, the form can't be processed

3 Have a great day

4 You, too

Mission **11** **Being Nominated for an Award**

Situation ❶

Ⓐ

1 He didn't receive an invitation to the year-end party.

2 It will take place at the Rosewood Lodge.

3 A comedian will perform after dinner.

4 She is collecting nominations for the employee of the year award.

Ⓑ

1 The Rosewood Lodge

2 7:00

3 December 28

4 speech

5 awards ceremony

6 standup

7 December 1

8 December 15

Background Knowledge

Ⓐ

1 It often includes an awards ceremony.

2 The employee with the best performance wins the award.

Ⓑ

> M Hi, Natasha. This is Kirk calling. As you know, the year-end party is at the Birch Center on December 27. The RSVP deadline was last Thursday. However, I haven't received yours. Please let me know by December 8 if you will attend. In addition, let me know if you're bringing a guest. Lastly, I'm still collecting nominations for the employee of the year award. I haven't received many nominations yet. So I wonder if you could nominate someone. Just send me an email with your RSVP and nomination. Thanks, Natasha.

1 a   **2** b   **3** c

Vocabulary

Ⓑ

1 invitation

2 employee of the year

3 RSVP

4 nominate

5 awards ceremony

6 acceptance speech

GRAMMAR

1 Can/contact   **2** can't turn on

3 can succeed   **4** can/use

5 can speak   **6** can/come

7 can attend   **8** can't fly

Situation ❷

Ⓐ

1 She received several nominations for the employee of the year award.

2 She will receive the award at the year-end party.

3 She will give an acceptance speech.

4 She should contact Gloria in Human Resources.

Useful Expressions

1 I'm really looking forward to it

2 Congratulations

3 It's such an honor

4 If you need some tips, Tammy can help you

12 Mission Resigning

Situation ❶

1 She wants to spend more time with her grandchildren.
2 She planned to leave in March.
3 It is currently understaffed.
4 The replacement should start in April.

B

1 April
2 recommend a few colleagues
3 the replacement
4 Annika
5 clients
6 May

Background Knowledge

A

1 It means you will leave your job two weeks after your announcement.
2 He or she might ask you to submit a written resignation letter.

B

M   Hi, Ms. Kim. Thanks for meeting with me.
W   No problem, Mr. Bell. What did you want to discuss?
M   Well, I'm planning to resign. I'd like to give my two weeks' notice.
W   I'm sorry to hear that. Can I encourage you to stay on for a few more months?
M   Unfortunately, no. I'm going to move overseas to be closer to my family.
W   I understand. Could you help us find a replacement?
M   Sure. I already have a few colleagues in mind.
W   Great. You can connect them with Mr. Benson in Human Resources. The sooner, the better.
M   Of course.

1 b   2 c   3 b

Vocabulary

B

1 d   2 b   3 a
4 d   5 a   6 d

1 to answer   2 to pay
3 to behave   4 to ask
5 to meet   6 to change
7 to buy   8 to email

Situation ❷

1 He messages her to ask how Martin is handling training.
2 He is having trouble with the company's computer system.
3 He will send him to the corporate office.
4 He might hand the smaller clients over to other staff members.

Useful Expressions

1 What sort of problems
2 I'm not sure I understand
3 Understandably, it is a lot to handle
4 That makes sense